Blossom Awakening

BLOSSOM AWAKENING

The Life and Poetry of Wandering Monk

SAIGYŌ

TRANSLATED BY

PETER LEVITT &
KAZUAKI TANAHASHI

SHAMBHALA

SHAMBHALA PUBLICATIONS, INC.
2129 13th Street
Boulder, Colorado 80302
www.shambhala.com

© 2025 by Peter Levitt and Kazuaki Tanahashi

Cover art: Kazuaki Tanahashi
Cover design: Kate E. White
Interior design: Lora Zorian

9 8 7 6 5 4 3 2 1

FIRST EDITION
Printed in the United States of America

Shambhala Publications makes every effort
to print on acid-free, recycled paper.
Shambhala Publications is distributed worldwide
by Penguin Random House, Inc., and its subsidiaries.

LIBRARY OF CONGRESS CATALOGING-IN-PUBLICATION DATA

Names: Saigyō, 1118–1190, author. | Levitt, Peter, translator. |
Tanahashi, Kazuaki, 1933– translator. | Saigyō, 1118–1190 Poems.
Selections. | Saigyō, 1118–1190 Poems. Selections. English.
Title: Blossom awakening: the life and poetry of wandering monk Saigyō /
translated by Peter Levitt and Kazuaki Tanahashi.
Description: First edition. | Boulder, Colorado: Shambhala, [2025] |
Includes bibliographical references and index.
Identifiers: LCCN 2024041681 | ISBN 9781645473633 (trade paperback)
Subjects: LCSH: Saigyō, 1118–1190—Translations into English. |
Waka—Translations into English. | LCGFT: Tanka. |
Biographies. | Literary criticism.
Classification: LCC PL788.5 .A2 2025 |
DDC 895.61/14—dc23/eng/20241231
LC record available at https://lccn.loc.gov/2024041681
The authorized representative in the EU for product safety and compliance
is eucomply oü, Pärnu mnt 139b-14, 11317 Tallinn, Estonia,
hello@eucompliancepartner.com.

To Samuel Bercholz
for his magnificent contribution
to spreading dharma in the Western world

Contents

Preface

It is our pleasure to present the life and work of Saigyō (1118–1190), one of Japan's most celebrated poets. Both of us fully enjoyed creating our last work, *The Complete Cold Mountain: Poems of the Legendary Hermit Hanshan*, to shed light on one of the peaks of Chinese literature. Now, we offer Saigyō's amazing poems for you to savor.

During Saigyō's early life, Norikiyo Satō, as Saigyō was then known, served the emperor's family as a low-class guard. This was at the end of the Heian period when elegant literature and the court culture were developed. His chosen poetic form from these early years until the end of his life was classical *waka*, written in five phrases of five, seven, five, seven, and seven syllables, which are best translated into five lines in English. More than two thousand poems by Saigyō are known to exist. Some of the poems have headnotes that reflect the background or context of their composition.

With this collection, we offer you Saigyō's *waka* poems on eleven themes, each with a brief introduction. For every one of the 193 poems in this book, we provide a number so the poem may easily be identified, its translation, the Japanese pronunciation, and the Japanese text, which combines ideographs (*kanji*) and phonetic symbols (*kana*). Enjoy!

—Peter Levitt and Kazuaki Tanahashi

Map of Japan
Provinces Related to Saigyō

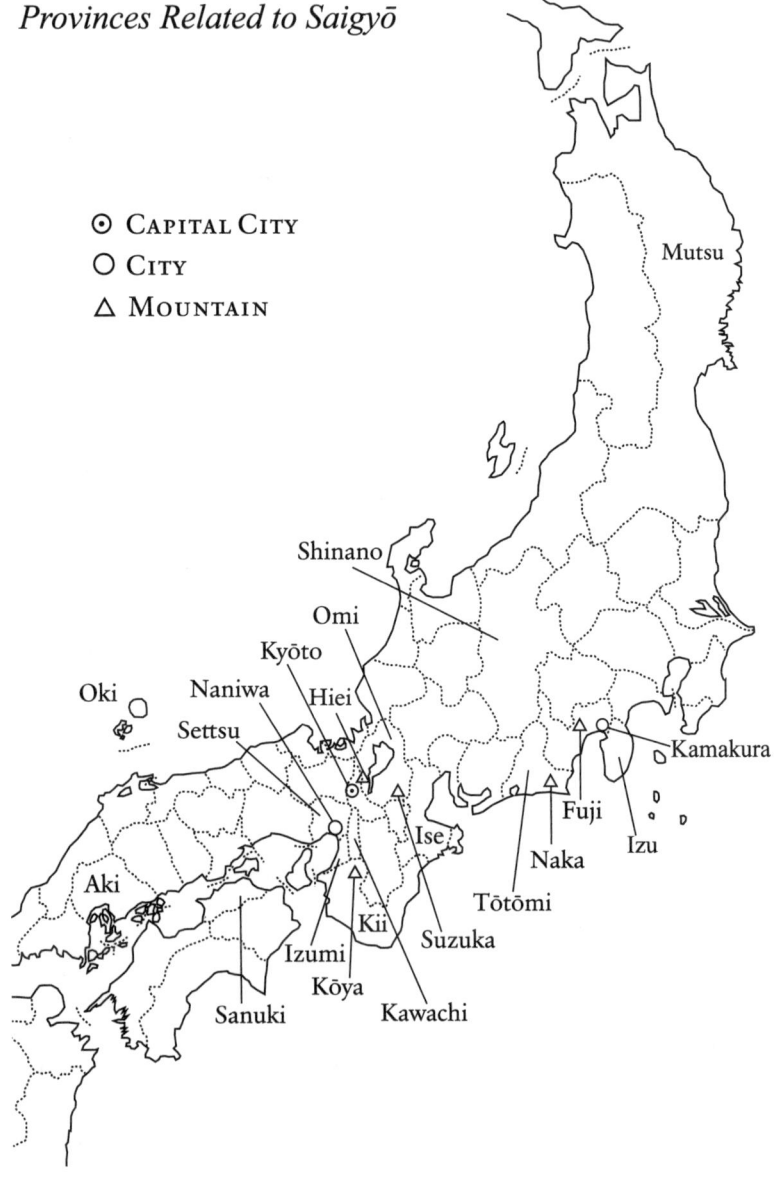

⊙ Capital City
○ City
△ Mountain

Mutsu

Shinano

Omi

Kyōto

Oki

Naniwa

Hiei

Settsu

Kamakura

Fuji

Izu

Ise

Naka

Aki

Tōtōmi

Kii

Izumi

Suzuka

Kōya

Sanuki

Kawachi

Chronology

Periods

Heian period: 749–1185
Kamakura period: 1185–1333

Emperors (on throne, dharma emperors)

Shirakawa: 1072–1086, 1086–1129
Horikawa: 1086–1107
Toba: 1107–1123, 1129–1156
Sutoku: 1123–1141
Konoe: 1141–1155
Goshirakawa: 1155–1158, 1158–1179, 1180–1192
Nijō: 1158–1165
Rokujō: 1165–1168
Takakura: 1168–1180, 1180
Antoku: 1180–1185
Gotoba: 1184–1198
Tsuchimikado: 1198–1210

Empresses (served; royal nuns)

Tamako: 1118–1123; Taikenmon'-in: 1124–1145
Tokuko: 1141–1155; Bifukumon'-in: 1155–1160
Tokushi: 1172–1180; Kenreimon'-in: 1185–1223

WARRIORS

Kiyomori Taira: 1118–1159 (prime minister: 1167)
Minamoto Yoritomo: 1147–1204 (*shōgun*: 1192–1204)

POETS

Toshinari (Shunzei) Fujiwara: 1114–1204
Monk Saigyō: 1118–1190
Sadaie (Teika) Fujiwara: 1162–1241
Taikenmon'-in Hyōe: d. 1183
Taikenmon'-in Horikawa: d. ?
Monk Saijū: d. 1173?
Monk Jien: 1155–1225

Blossom Awakening

INTRODUCTION

Viewing cherry blossoms in their prime under a full moon was so sublime that sadness overtook him. An erotic encounter with someone high above the clouds was exuberant to the point of tragedy. So sorrowful, so heartbroken, so full of *aware*—a Japanese word conveying pathos, aesthetics, poesy, and the fullness of existence—this was the life of the wanderer Saigyō (1118–1190). His poetic form was *waka*, also called *tanka*—a one-column poem consisting of phrases of five, seven, five, seven, and seven syllables, usually translated into five lines. Though he was not well known while he was alive, Saigyō had occasion to exchange poems with a former emperor, onetime court ladies, and renowned poets.

While most of the recognized poets of his time were members of the imperial court who composed their verses from their imaginations, as a Buddhist monk Saigyō had the freedom to journey to actual poetic sites, live in nature, and write from his own experience. This was fully appreciated by his contemporaries—soon after his death, ninety-four of Saigyō's poems were included in the *Shinkokin Waka Shū* (*New Ancient and Present Waka Collection*), the most prestigious anthology of the era. It was the largest number of poems by any poet in the collection. Later on, his stories were adopted by the Noh theater, which made him legendary.

LIFE IN TIMES OF TURMOIL

Saigyō lived through a dramatic time of tumult and social upheaval. In twelfth-century Japan, political maneuvering, abuse of the dharma by the ruling family in Kyōto, incest, and infant emperorship all led to the rapid decline of the monarchy and the end of three and a half centuries of peace. This resulted in a takeover by the warrior class, a profound shift in power and culture that brought an end to the Heian (Kyōto) period (794–1185) and marked the beginning of the Kamakura period (1185–1333). Saigyō likely foresaw the fighting among rulers and soldier clans that would characterize this period, and he wanted freedom from all actions associated with possessiveness, power, and violence. Thus, he became a samurai who denounced the sword.

Later, Saigyō wrote a headnote to a poem: "In this world, soldiers have raised their armies, and there is no place without battles west and east, north and south. The number of people being killed is continuously enormous. It is unbelievable indeed. Wondering what on earth they fight for, and feeling what pitiful sights there are, I have written this poem:

> There is no end
> to people
> starting across the mountain of death—
> the number of those killed
> keeps growing.

Then he added ridiculing words: "The soldiers alone seem to be crossing the mountain toward death. But they don't need to be afraid of robbers as those who are armed would feel safe in this world." An early antiwar poem of Japan.

From Sword to Monk's Cane

In 1140, Norikiyo Satō, as Saigyō was known at the time, went to see Dharma Emperor Toba,* whom Norikiyo had been serving as a guard, to get permission to resign and depart the court. The warrior Norikiyo presented this poem:

> Though I hold this world
> dear, I cannot remain
> attached—
> only by forsaking the self
> can I be free.

This formal resignation request would pave the way for Nori-kiyo's new vocation as a monk. He was twenty-three years old, and Toba was thirty-four. This event was seen as rather shocking in the imperial court. Although Norikiyo was a low-class officer, Yorinaga Fujiwara, who later became a prime minister, noted in his journal:

> Saigyō was originally Lieutenant Norikiyo. As an ac-complished soldier from generations of a warrior family, he was serving Dharma Emperor Toba. He had an aspiration for the buddha way during his time of laity. He was young, from a well-to-do family, and had

---

* Toba was referred to in this way as he had abdicated his throne but was ruling as a priest.

nothing to worry about. Nevertheless, he escaped from the world. People admire it.

Serving in the palace was a distinct privilege. The capital city of Kyōto was established in 794. The grid plan of the city centered on the palace, following that of the capital city of Chang'an in Tang dynasty China. An elegant culture producing accomplished poetry and music had flourished in Kyōto for over three hundred years. The royal family was assisted by members of the aristocratic Fujiwara clan, who occupied major administrative positions, often allowing the clan's girls to marry into the royal family. All those in the court wished to retain their positions and strive for higher ranks. Therefore, people wondered why Norikiyo abruptly left the palace.

A historical account called *Gempei Seisui Ki* (Record of the Rise and Fall of Genji and Heike [Minamoto and Taira] Clans) mentions Norikiyo's departure from the secular world:

Now, if we look into the rise of his aspiration for enlightenment, it is understood that its cause was love. He fell in love with—without revealing the name of—a highest-ranking lady, and was commanded, "This is a matter of Akogi Bay." He therefore gave up his love, realizing that a higher official rank is an impossible fantasy of a spring evening, while pleasure and prosperity are like the moon setting in the west. So he escaped from his commitment to the world of purpose and entered the path beyond boundary.

Akogi Bay on the Ise Peninsula is known for fishing that is allowed only once a year, so "a matter of Akogi Bay" is a poetic expression meaning "just once and no more." If we look at Saigyō's desperate love and longing throughout his poetic career, including the following verse, the preceding account becomes rather convincing:

> Knowing my place,
> I realize it's not her fault,
> and yet—
> pressed against my resentful face,
> my sleeves are wet with tears.

Hideo Takahashi asserts in his 1993 book *Saigyō* that Saigyō's love interest was a woman named Taikenmon'-in. This was a retired royal title of Empress Tamako, who was also called Shōshi (1101–1145). Seventeen years older than Norikiyo, Tamako was the youngest daughter of Kinzane Fujiwara, a member of a high aristocratic family whom Norikiyo's family—noted for their mastery of archery—had served for generations. Thus, Norikiyo knew her, and after becoming Saigyō, he would still engage in frequent poetic correspondence with ladies serving Tamako.

At age five, Tamako had been adopted by Dharma Emperor Shirakawa (1053–1129), who was the first monarch in the Retired Emperor period—the time when retired emperors actually ruled instead of the emperors on the throne. Retiring emperors typically chose their oldest sons to occupy the throne even if they were very young children. Some of the retired emperors of the Heian period were called cloistered or dharma emperors, as they took formal Buddhist vows as monks after abdicating. However, they maintained their power and influence, in effect giving up only ceremonial duties.

Shirakawa was on the throne between the ages of twenty and thirty-four (1073–1087), then became absolute dictator as the dharma emperor for forty-two years (1087–1129). He listed only three things that were out of his control: the flow of the Kamo River (which runs through Kyōto), spots on a die, and monk warriors. Shirakawa, fifty-three years older, made Tamako his mistress when she was in her early teens. Later, wanting her to have a good marriage, he offered her in marriage to a son of the regent, Tadazane Fujiwara. But Tadazane found a way to delay acceptance of the offer. In his journal, he confided:

> The princess of the Dharma Emperor is a lover of Sue-michi (Fujiwara), governor of Bingo Province. People in the world all know this. What an incomprehensible matter! . . . The princess also is having an affair with a novice of Zōken, the precept master of the palace. How strange! This is a matter of the End Times.

As this marriage did not take place, Shirakawa decided to marry Tamako to his grandson, Toba. Toba had ascended to the throne at age five in 1107, after the death of his father, Horikawa. He married Tamako in 1118, when he was sixteen and Tamako eighteen. Even after their marriage, Shirakawa asked her to see him quite often and kept her as one of his many courtesans for decades. When Tamako was going to give birth to her first child, Shirakawa ordered Buddhist monastics to hold elaborate rituals for her safe delivery. A prince, to become Emperor Sutoku at the age of five, was born to Tamako in 1119, when Norikiyo was two years old. Tamako's husband, Toba, was fully aware that Sutoku was his grandfather's child; he sarcastically referred to Sutoku as his uncle's son. This was no secret in the court.

During the reign of Toba from 1107 to 1123, and after he became a retired emperor, the royal love triangle—Shirakawa, Toba, and Tamako—often staged magnificent parades on carriages and horseback, accompanied by dressed-up courtiers, to visit renowned sites in the city. On one occasion, Norikiyo happened to be selected to serve as a guard—a great honor.

Tamako, an enchanting beauty and noted harp player, surrounded by the sexual extravagance of Shirakawa and having to compete with other women in order to attract him, was a woman of erotic mastery with the highest authority. She was attended by ladies who were part of her conspiracy, because nobody—not even her lover or husband—had control over her amorous life. A free woman indeed. Tamako's illicit union with Norikiyo was perhaps a mere casual pastime for her, which she might have engaged in with other attractive young men of whom she took note in the court. But for Norikiyo, much more was at stake: by having a carnal relationship with his lord's wife, he was at risk of being punished by death for committing adultery and treason.

The affair was likely to have taken place around 1140. In 1123, Dharma Emperor Shirakawa deposed his twenty-one-year-old grandson, Toba, and enthroned Sutoku, his own five-year-old son. After Shirakawa's death, Toba became the dharma emperor. Sutoku's mother, Tamako, became the former empress at age twenty-three and received the retired royal title Taikenmon'-in the following year. Shirakawa died in 1129 at age seventy-seven, when Norikiyo was twelve years old. Toba fell in love with the fourteen-years-younger Nariko (also called Tokushi) Fujiwara, from a low aristocratic family, who gave birth to his son, prince-to-be Konoe in 1139. It would be fitting that this was the time of Tamako and Norikiyo's affair; in the following year, Toba pushed Tamako away and made Nariko empress.

As he revealed in his farewell poem to Dharma Emperor Toba, Norikiyo became a home leaver to be free of the entangled, unethical, and unequal relationship that left him in fear of being destroyed. Tamako must have been well aware of Norikiyo's intention, and Toba may have suspected it and forgiven him as well.

There is no record of how Norikio was ordained as Monk Saigyō, by whom or in which school of Buddhism. Zen had not yet reached Japan at this time. The belief in going to the Pure Land in the west after death by chanting the name of Amitābha Buddha was gaining popularity, although Pure Land schools had not yet been established. From his name, which translates as "going west," as well as through his poems, it may be safe to assume that Saigyō was immersed in Pure Land chanting. Also, from his earliest location as a monk, he must have been associated with Mount Hiei, the center of the Tendai School. Later he became a priest of the Shingon (Mantra) School. Tendai and Shingon were the main schools of Buddhism in the Heian period.

Saigyō remained in his hometown of Kyōto for some time, trying to figure out his future away from home, wondering:

Should I dye
my heart
the pure color of the moon—
while I'm not leaving
the capital?

In 1142, two years after Norikiyo's departure from the palace, Former Empress Tamako became a nun at age forty-two in the presence of Toba and Sutoku at Hōkongō Temple, which she had built as part of the large Ninna Temple compound, Omuro village, west of Kyōto. In that year, Saigyō moved to Kurama, a village northeast of Kyōto at the foot of Mount Hiei, the headquarters of the Tendai School. This Mahāyāna Buddhist school was established in Japan in 806 by the monk Saichō (767–822). Based on the Chinese Tiantai School, it taught a comprehensive form of Buddhism, consisting of Mahāyāna precepts, the Lotus Sūtra, tantric practice, and meditation. Scores of Tendai halls and huts were scattered over the landscape. Saigyō thought he had abandoned all desires and attachment to comfort, but in early winter, when water stopped coming to his hut, he reflected,

It makes no sense,
I thought I'd given up everything—
now that water is frozen
in the bamboo pipe,
I long for spring.

Awakened with Blossoms

Soon Saigyō traveled east, then south to visit Ise Province, the location of the Grand (Shintō) Shrine, the sanctuary of the sun goddess Amaterasu. Like most other Japanese, Saigyō had a dual faith—in Shintōism, the indigenous religion, and in Buddhism, which originated in India and was transmitted to Japan through China and Korea. Mount Suzuka was on the way to Ise. Following the random will of his traveling cane, his heart was filled with not-knowing:

> Mount Suzuka,
> since I've cast away
> this floating world—
> what will become
> of my life?

Not-knowing, but not not-feeling. So much love, longing, and aching are in the poet's heart, in the cane he used during his journeys, and in his brush.

> Since the wind carries
> so many tender feelings
> through the treetops—
> I know it is autumn
> in this deep mountain village.

Scores of miles to the west of Ise spreads Mount Yoshino in Kii Province, the most celebrated site in poetry for viewing stunning scenes of wild cherry blossoms. Saigyō hummed,

Scattering the heart of one
who can't bear parting—
the spring mountain breeze
entices
cherry petals away.

For Saigyō, viewing the blossoms was no longer cherishing
and enjoying them alone, but a communion with blossoms. Sep-
aration between subject and object disappeared, and his heart
became the fragrance and splendor of petals. The moon for
Saigyō was also his adored one, his love, his heart. Being in na-
ture is to be awakened with nature; to be nature itself.

In 1144, at age twenty-seven, our poet journeyed toward the
northeast and reached Mutsu Province (present-day Iwate Pre-
fecture) on the Main Island. He wanted to visit esteemed poetic
sites. Courtiers in the royal residence would imagine such loca-
tions for poetic composition, but Saigyō wanted to be at the ac-
tual sites to make his experience and inspirations real.

On his way, Saigyō was told that one outstanding tombstone
was for an ancient poet, Sanekata Fujiwara (?–999), so he noted,

The poet's name alone
has not decayed—
I see this dried up field
of pampas grass
as his memorial.

The wandering was not easy:

When snow falls,
burying the paths
of mountains and fields
beneath the sky of my journey,
I can't tell here from there.

He also wrote:

With the roaring sound,
how could my heart
not become clear?
Grasses and trees bow down
in the storm.

After his return to Kii Province around 1149, he did not live on
Mount Hiei but found instead a hut on Mount Kōya in a moun-
tainous area about seventy-five miles southeast of the capital city.
Saigyō resided on the mountain on and off for three decades. This
sacred mountain had been chosen by Kūkai, Great Master Kōbō
(774–835), in 816 as the headquarters and training center of the
Shingon School, a major Japanese school of esoteric Vajrayāna
Buddhism known for its intricate rituals of reverence for complex
pantheons of buddhas and bodhisattvas. During the time Saigyō
lived on Mount Kōya, it was widely believed that Great Master
Kōbō was still meditating in the inner sanctuary of this monastic
compound.

In 1145 Former Empress Tamako passed away at age forty-
five. Saigyō, at age twenty-eight, sent a note of condolence to
Horikawa, one of Tamako's ladies:

Even if we asked,
the wind
could not tell us where
she has gone—
the one who fell like a flower.

Horikawa answered back indicating that she would follow her majesty wherever she might be:

If the blowing wind
would let me know
where she has gone—
I would not wait
to fall like a flower.

Struggles in the Royal Family

In the year 1141, Toba forced his "uncle's son," Sutoku, to step down from the throne and replaced him with his own son, Konoe, who was three years old. Sutoku, now age twenty-three, was given the unusual title of *kōtaitei* (crown brother), which prohibited him from becoming a retired-emperor ruler. This left Sutoku feeling resentful and, secretly, he vowed revenge.

Sutoku loved poetry and commanded Akisuke Fujiwara to compile an imperial *waka* book called *Shika Shū* (*Word Blossom Collection*), which was completed in 1151. One of Saigyō's poems was included:

Do those who
renounce the self,
truly renounce?
Not renouncing
is, indeed, renouncing!

But because Saigyō was formerly a low-class officer, the author of his poem was listed as Anonymous.

Konoe died in 1155, and Goshirakawa, a biological son of Toba and Tamako, acceded to the throne at age twenty-nine. Former Emperor Toba passed away on the second day of the seventh month in 1156 at age fifty-four after being on the throne for sixteen years and ruling as dharma emperor for twenty-seven. Saigyō, then age thirty-nine and still living on Mount Kōya, happened to visit Kyōto and saw his majesty's body being taken to the palace. Saigyō participated in the simple funeral and chanted *sūtras* all through the night. He was grief-stricken and touched, remembering the past:

> Only this evening
> do I realize
> it was not shallow—
> my closeness
> with the Lord.

Nine days after Toba's death, the former emperor Sutoku and his army, a mixture of Minamoto and Taira guards, attacked Emperor Goshirakawa's forces on the eleventh day of the seventh month. This is called the battle of the Hōgen era. Easily defeated, Sutoku ran into his brother's Ninna Temple and shaved his head on the fourteenth day of the month.

Saigyō, who had an affinity with the first son of Empress Tamako, who was only a year younger than himself, went to see Sutoku at the temple. A Shingon priest came out to meet Saigyō. In this catastrophic situation, the moon was bright and clear. That saddened him even further:

Even in such a world,
the moon's clear light
doesn't change—
yet I resent
that I still see it.

The punishment was severe for those who fought for Sutoku. The shore of the River Kamo in the capital city was full of executed bodies. A commander of the Minamoto clan on the victorious side was ordered to decapitate even his own father, a commander of Sutoku's army. On the twenty-third day of the same month, Sutoku was sent into exile with three ladies-in-waiting in Sanuki Province on Shikoku Island.

By and by, one of these anonymous ladies-in-waiting wrote to Saigyō for Sutoku. Though he did not sign the communication, it was clearly from him:

There is no way
for it to flow
through my brush—
please draw out
the feelings in my heart.

Saigyō comforted the exiled one:

Though far away,
only hearts
can express it—
please let a trace flow
through your brush.

Sutoku copied five scriptures with his own blood and asked Goshirakawa's government to allow him to offer them to a temple in Kyōto, but the government, suspicious of a curse that might be harbored in the calligraphy, rejected his request. Sutoku was enraged and swore to become a demon and haunt the royal court. Sutoku died in 1164 at age forty-six. Three years after that, Saigyō visited the Matsuyama (Pine Mountain) Port area and looked for the remains of Sutoku's residence-in-exile but could find no traces. He wrote in consolation to Sutoku's wrathful spirit:

> The appearance of waves
> at Pine Mountain
> hasn't changed—
> but you have become
> beyond form.

The Emergence of Warrior Regimes

Kiyomori Taira, a former colleague of Norikiyo, was also the same age. He was a guard to Dharma Emperor Toba. As the head of the large Taira clan, Kiyomori was a powerful figure. The commander of the forces that defeated Sutoku, he was trusted by Emperor Goshirakawa. In 1159, an armed uprising called the battle of the Heiji era was attempted but quickly subjugated. Until then, the Taira clan—based in the western provinces—and the Minamoto clan—from the eastern provinces—together had been guards to the imperial palaces. But in this battle, major Minamoto soldiers were killed or exiled. Consequently, Kiyomori seized control of all the military and police forces in the capital city and was admitted to the court for the first time as a samurai.

Goshirakawa abdicated the throne at age thirty-two in favor of his eight-year-old son, Nijō. Thus, Goshirakawa started his own dharma emperorship, which lasted for over thirty years with some interruptions. Kiyomori finalized the construction of Renge-ō (Lotus King) Tendai Temple where, in 1165, images of a majestic one-thousand-armed Avalokiteshvara were enshrined in a villa belonging to Goshirakawa. (Today it is known as Sanjūsangen-dō and contains one thousand sculptures of Avalokiteshvara, completed around 1265.) Kiyomori earned unprecedentedly swift promotion and was appointed prime minister (the highest-ranking courtier) in 1167 at age fifty. He fell ill and retired from his official position the following year, when he became a priest but kept the power to govern. In the same year, he finished renovating a breathtaking group of buildings, including a large vermilion torii standing on the inland sea at Itsukushima Shrine on Miyajima Island (in present-day Hiroshima Prefecture).

To maintain an intimate relationship with Kiyomori, Goshirakawa arranged for his son Emperor Takakura (age twelve) to marry Kiyomori's daughter Tokushi (age sixteen) in 1172. As a result, Kiyomori's family members received high standing in court.

During this time, Saigyō likely remained in the hut on Mount Kōya. In 1174 he wrote a letter to the mountain community, encouraging them to recite the magical incantation "supreme (Buddha's) head *dharani*" one million times for Kiyomori in return for the latter's favor of exempting tax for construction of a Shintō shrine in Kii. It seems that Saigyō contacted his old comrade and pleaded with him to relieve the Shingon Buddhist community from the financial burden.

Kiyomori had expanded a trade route with Song dynasty China through the port of Fukuhara (present-day Kobe) and secured prosperity for the nation, while also accumulating wealth for the Taira clan. Goshirakawa became concerned about Kiyomori's growing influence and exerted his own authority to suppress Kiyomori's leadership, but in 1179 Kiyomori fired a great number of courtiers who were against him, placed Goshirakawa under palace arrest, and dissolved the latter's rulership. In 1180 Emperor Takakura descended the throne at age twenty and enthroned his four-year-old son, Antoku. Kiyomori attempted to maintain complete dominance in the government behind the nominal reign of Dharma Emperor Takakura, his son-in-law. Ultimately the imperial family lost its power, and full military rule under Kiyomori commenced. Some people believed that this upset was a result of the vengeful Sutoku's demonic influence.

In the same year, Prince Mochihito, the third son of Goshirakawa, issued a nationwide appeal to attack and destroy Kiyomori. Some Minamoto and other fighters responded and raised armies in the eastern and other parts of the country. In 1181, monk soldiers of Onjō Monastery, east of Kyōto, and Kōfuku Monastery in Nara also raised troops against Kiyomori. As a result, fighting broke out all over. Kiyomori's army burned Onjō Monastery, as well as Tōdai Monastery, the temple of the Great Buddha statue, and Kōfuku Monastery in Nara. This is the time

Saigyō was speaking of when he grieved the battles being fought all over Japan.

Kiyomori died of a high fever in 1181 at age sixty-four. In 1185 the five-year-old emperor's mother, Tokushi, received the retired royal title of Kenreimon'-in.

Yoshinaka Minamoto from the region of Kiso, Shinano Province, advanced his army and was poised to seize Kyōto in 1183. Goshirakawa escaped to Mount Hiei. All Taira soldiers vacated the city and rushed westward, guarding Emperor Antoku and Kenreimon'-in. Yoshinaka occupied Kyōto, but a famine was already devastating the city, with houses being vacated and destroyed. Maintaining a large military operation strained the city so that crime became impossible to control. In the following year, Goshirakawa installed Takakura's son Gotoba as emperor at age four. Now Japan had two emperors—Antoku in the west and Gotoba in Kyōto. Yoshinaka, a wild, uncultivated soldier from the countryside, had no clue how to deal with royalty and high-ranking courtiers. Goshirakawa, who came to predict a total defeat of the Taira clan, had to make a choice between the two rival Minamoto forces competing for the power to rule the nation. Eventually, instead of choosing Yoshinaka, he ordered Yoritomo Minamoto, based in Izu Province near Mount Fuji, to attack the Taira armies. At one point, Yoshinaka imprisoned Goshirakawa and reinforced his own waning popularity.

Yoritomo's troops approached Kyōto and killed Yoshinaka in 1184. Saigyō heard about it and wrote of Yoshinaka—the man from Kiso—without sympathy:

A man from Kiso
couldn't drop anchor
in the raging sea—
he entered
the mountain of death.

The Taira armies, commanded by poets and musicians dec-
orated at court, were no match for the well-trained Minamoto
soldiers. After losing all their battles, they boarded boats in Dan-
no-ura Bay, between the two peninsulas of Main Island and
Kyūshū Island. At the final naval battle in 1185, all remaining
fighters, as well as the eight-year-old Emperor Antoku and his
grandmother Tokiko (Kiyomori's widow), all drowned at sea.
Thus, the Taira clan vanished.

Only Emperor Antoku's mother, Kenreimon'-in, was res-
cued and secluded herself in a small hermitage in the village of
Ohara, north of Kyōto. The chapter "Imperial Visit to Ohara" in
Heike Monogatari (*Tale of Heike* [Taira Clan]) describes a call paid
by Former Emperor Goshirakawa to his daughter-in-law. This
episode is a climax of the great Buddhist epic, which was sung
by blind monks playing a Heike *biwa* (lute). As a daughter of the
most powerful and richest man in the country, having the em-
peror as her husband and her infant child as crown prince, she'd
had all the glory in the world. Now, having lost everything, she
was living in a humble shed. Yet, according to the narrative, she
was the one who had a glimpse of *nirvāna*.

If he had remained in his position, the warrior Norikiyo
would have fought for Former Emperor Sutoku amid the chaos
and battles that lasted almost three decades. He easily could

have been injured or killed. Norikiyo/Saigyō had an affinity with Sutoku because the latter was the first son of Empress Tamako, whom the former warrior adored, and also a great supporter of poetry. If Norikiyo had been fortunate, he might have served Kiyomori, eventually been defeated, and strayed into the countryside. Because he became a monk, as expressed in his farewell poem to Dharma Emperor Toba, he was able to "save" himself. Being a mendicant of no rank, Saigyō had the freedom of not taking sides in war, enabling him to correspond with people in all quarters and deepen his practice as a poet and a monk.

After driving out the Taira armies, Yoritomo Minamoto appointed governors to all provinces in 1185. He was made *shōgun*, a feudal role of commander-in-chief, and established a government in Kamakura in 1192, marking the end of the Heian period and the beginning of the Kamakura period.

In 1186, Saigyō, at age sixty-nine, volunteered to help the priest Chōgen, who had begun to repair the Great Buddha Statue of the Tōdai Temple in Nara. They needed donations of massive amounts of alluvial gold to gild the surface of the Great Buddha's body. (Only its face and head had been gilded by that time.) Saigyō headed north to talk with the wealthy Hidehira Fujiwara, who was based in Hiraizumi in Mutsu Province.

On his way, remembering his first journey forty-two years before, he was nostalgic:

> After so many years,
> how could I have imagined?
> What a life!
> Once again crossing
> the middle mountains of Saya.

Middle Mountain (Nakayama) in Saya (present-day Shizuoka Prefecture) is near Mount Fuji, which was erupting. Shortly after that, in Kamakura, Saigyō met with Yoritomo Minamoto, soon to be appointed the first *shōgun* of the military government, to secure the transport of bags of gold. Consequently, enough gold was delivered to Nara in that year to complete the repair of the statue. Saigyō, after completing his mission, returned to his hut in 1187. (The construction of Great Buddha Hall was completed in 1190.)

POETIC RELATIONS

For most of his life after becoming a home leaver, Saigyō lived and traveled alone. But he had a dharma brother called Saijū, who was perhaps ten or more years older.* They had formerly been samurai of compatible ranks. Both became Shingon priests, practicing and traveling together at times. Once Saigyō wrote from Mount Kōya to Saijū, who was in Kyōto:

> For no particular reason,
> I keep longing for you
> as I cross the bridge—
> moonlight is
> my only rival.

Saijū sent back his love:

> Without seeing
> what's in my heart
> as I think of you—

* Saigyō means "west going" and Saijū "west abiding."

only moonlight is your rival
as you cross the bridge.

While they were traveling together in Shikoku in 1167, Saijū had to return to Kyōto. He passed away around 1173, to Saigyō's devastation.

Saigyō also corresponded with the ladies serving Taikenmon'-in (Tamako). Among them, Hyōe (?–1183) and her elder sister Horikawa (dates unknown) were noted poets. They must have been fully aware of his past affair with the former empress. When Saigyō heard that Taikenmon'-in's daughter Tōshi (Former Empress Jōsaimon'-in) had to cancel a cherry blossom viewing due to rain, Saigyō wrote to then-lady-in-waiting, Hyōe, reflecting on the time when Taikenmon'-in was in power.

> For those who see them,
> blossoms also must
> be thinking of the past—
> their longing
> withered by rain.

Hyōe, who had been sought for her beauty in the past, confided her feelings about old age and loneliness:

> Who would
> see the rain
> and long for the past?
> Flowers also have no companions
> from those days.

Saigyō had promised to visit Lady Horikawa, who had become a nun in 1142 with Taikenmon'-in at Ninna Temple, but he failed to do so for some time. Hearing of his having passed in front of the temple gate, she noted with resentment:

> I depended on moonlight
> to guide me
> traveling west—
> how disappointing
> to trust in vain!

Saigyō countered with this poem, stating without apology but with humor:

> Not shining through,
> moonlight
> avoided the clouds—
> it saw your heart
> wasn't waiting in the sky.

All of these poems appeared in Saigyō's main collection of *waka* poems, *Sanka Shū* (*Mountain Abode Collection*).

Once Saigyō visited Shitennō Temple in Naniwa (present-day Ōsaka). This sanctuary enshrines the Four Deva Kings of the cardinal directions; it was also known that people could have a vision of the Pure Land from its western gate. One day while he was passing a pleasure quarter called Eguchi on the broad Yodo River, it started raining heavily. Saigyō asked a prostitute to give him temporary shelter, but she declined. So he teased,

To abandon the world
one must be firm—
but you must be just as certain,
not sharing this shelter
for a little while.

Surprisingly, the woman replied,

Hearing you are
a home leaver—
I hope
you're not attached
to this temporary abode!

This dialogue between an unusual couple, a monk and a prostitute, was included in his *Sanka Shū* as well as in a prominent anthology *Shinkokin Waka Shū* (*New Ancient and Present Waka Collection*).

Saigyō heard that Toshinari (Shunzei) Fujiwara had been put in charge of compiling an imperial selection of poems called *Senzai Waka Shū* (*One-Thousand-Year Waka Collection*) under the command of Dharma Emperor Goshirakawa in 1183. He humbly wrote to Toshinari, the most prestigious poet of that time, who was four years younger than himself:

Although these words
are not flowers,
you might pick one,

to see the color
it holds inside

Toshinari graciously replied:

In the words of one
who left the world
to enter the way—
the color of deep feelings
is clear.

Toshinari selected eighteen of Saigyō's poems, placing his name in an imperial anthology for the first time.

In 1180, Saigyō moved to Ise Province at the age of sixty-three. In 1187, he concluded *Mimosuso Gawa Utaawase* (*Mimosuso River Waka Duals*). Mimosuso is another name for the Isuzu River, running beside the Ise Grand Shrine. Saigyō created a format of dual *waka* poems with his own works. The anthology consisted of thirty-six pairs of poems. He asked Toshinari to be the juror. (Usually dual *waka* competitions were contests between different poets, but Saigyō had never participated in such a competition.) Toshinari chose the winning poems, judging some of the duals a draw, with thoughtful comments. One of the poems in this collection is:

From the serene clouds
over Vulture Peak,
moonlight
softens
in Tsukiyomi Forest.

Here you see a merging of Shintōism, the native Japanese animistic faith, and Buddhism. According to scriptures, Vulture Peak in the kingdom of Magadha, northeastern India, is where Shākyamuni Buddha gave sermons. Tsukiyomi, the moon god, is the brother of Amaterasu, goddess of the sun and universe. Tsukiyomi Forest refers to the Tsukiyomi Shrine, a sub-shrine of the Grand Shrine of Ise. "Moonlight softens" means that a buddha or bodhisattva conceals the light of enlightenment and emerges as a local deity to save those who are suffering.

In 1189, at age seventy-two, Saigyō finalized another collection of duals titled *Miyagawa Utaawase* (*Shrine River Duals*). It also consisted of thirty-six pairs of his own poems. This time he asked Sadaie (Teika) Fujiwara (1162–1241), who was Toshinari's son, to be the juror. Sadaie would become a leading poet of his time, participating in the compilation of two imperial anthologies—*Shinkokin Waka Shū* (*New Ancient and Present Waka Collection*) and *Shin Chokusen Waka Shū* (*New Imperial Waka Collection*)—as well as *Ogura Hyakunin Isshu* (*Ogura Collection of One Hundred Poems by One Hundred Poets*), the most popular anthology ever in Japan. He would also write books on poetics, including *Kindai Shūka* (*Excellent Poems in Recent Times*). But Sadaie was only twenty-eight years old when Saigyō approached him; it was a towering challenge for him to comment on poems by Saigyō, a far more senior literary figure. Sadaie struggled to present the result of his endeavor in 1189, a year before Saigyō's death. Overjoyed at receiving the younger man's laborious work, Saigyō wrote to him,

I was delighted feeling that this was brought by a messenger of the Goddess (of Ise). I immediately looked at it three times. Then I asked someone to read it three times, which I heard while sobbing. And yet, I was not sure, so I pushed myself up from bed and read it in two days.

Then Saigyō asked his priest friend Jien to make a clean copy of the anthology with Teika's comments so it could be presented to the Grand Shrine of Ise.

Previously, Jien, thirty-seven years younger than Saigyō and a brother of the regent Kanezane Fujiwara, had asked Saigyō to teach him a mantra of the Tendai School. Saigyō had replied that the mantra could not be mastered without studying *waka*. So Jien studied it and asked Saigyō again.

In 1181, Jien ordained Shinran, at age nine, the future founder of the Jōdo Shin (Pure Land True) School. Jien, soon to be one of the prominent poets himself, would become the head of the Tendai School four times. He would oppose Dharma Emperor Gotoba's raising an army against the Hōjō troops, a newly rising warrior clan.

In 1189 Saigyō and Jien visited Mudō Temple on the east side of Mount Hiei, the base for a rigorous, thousand-day marathon practice by Tendai monks. By the end, they would run or briskly walk the equivalent of circumambulating the equator. Jien had completed this hard practice thirteen years before. Looking down at Lake Biwa in Ōmi Province, Saigyō said, "I have stopped composing poems for some time but let me try something now," and recited,

Grebes shining in the sun,
the lake calm
in the morning—
when I look far off,
a boat leaving no trace behind.

Jien harmonized,

In the faint light,
no trace of a boat
rowing on Ōmi Lake—
my heart
will follow that way.

Toward the Pure Land

Saigyō moved to Saga Village, in the western suburbs of Kyōto, in 1187. It is just west of the royal Ninna Temple in the Omuro area, where Tamako and her first son Sutoku had become ordained, each of them heartbroken. Once, joining a gathering where people wrote humorous poems, Saigyō made fun of himself:

A bamboo horse—
today I lean on it
as a cane,
remembering
childhood games.

It appears that he saw his life approaching its end:

The lamp also
loses the strength
to shine—
I'll just wait
until its light comes to an end.

Buddhism was in decline at the time. Large monasteries were secularized as the high priesthood was occupied by the aristocracy, while lower-class practitioners formed monk-warrior battalions that resorted to violence. There was a prevalent belief that, more than one thousand years after the *pari-nirvāna* (death) of Shākyamuni Buddha, Buddhism had entered *mappō*, the age of declined dharma, when no more true practice or enlightenment was available. Fearing that there was no salvation in this defiled world, people looked for awakening after death in the Pure Land. Chanting the name of Amitābha Buddha, who was believed to reside in the western paradise, became the sole practice. Bishop Genshin (942–1017) of the Tendai School was the most prominent advocate of this practice.

Saigyō, quoting Genshin's words, wrote in a headnote, followed by a poem:

When you are focused on the Buddha's name, a lotus will grow in the western world. If you do not retreat from this practice throughout life, this flower will come and welcome you.

I let the flower of my heart
go before me
to the pond of the western land—
without forgetting this,
I await the teaching of dharma.

Another poem on Saigyō's Pure Land belief goes like this:

A bliss of sacred beings welcomes (the diseased) to the Pure Land:
Dying my heart
with its color
in a single stroke—
a purple cloud
spreads above.

Saigyō seemed to have reached a positive state of mind regarding death:

When I resolve
to die
calmly—
my heart
echoes, Yes!

For Saigyō, death was not a moment of dread, but a moment of splendor. It was the beginning of a new journey to the west. He wanted his death surrounded by utter beauty—bright moonlight and cherry blossoms. So he exclaimed,

How I wish
I could die
beneath cherry blossoms—
in the middle of spring
when the moon is full.

In Japanese, the poetic name for the second month in the lunar calendar is *kisaragi*, meaning "clothes adding," as it is still cold. A full moon takes place on the fifteenth day of each month. In Mahāyāna Buddhism, the fifteenth day of the second month is believed to be when Shākyamuni Buddha entered *pari-nirvāna*.

Saigyō wrote this poem when he was active as a poet. He sent it to Toshinari Fujiwara, who started to edit *Senzai Shū* in 1183 and completed it in 1188, with this poem included. That means it was written around the time Saigyō was sixty-six years old and became widely known when he was seventy-one.

In 1190, when Saigyō was seventy-three years old, he became ill in his hut at Hirokawa (Wide River) Temple in Kawachi Province (east of present-day Ōsaka) at the foot of Mount Katsuragi, not far from the Yamato River. Perhaps he was aware that the conclusion of his life was drawing near. He fasted with great determination and passed away on the sixteenth day of the second month, under a full moon surrounded by cherry blossoms blooming in their prime, as he had wished. Dying in this way was his last poetic expression.

Monk Jien heard about the passing of Saigyō (also called En'i) and wrote,

Venerable En'i passed away at the Sheep Hour (roughly two in the afternoon) of the sixteenth day of the second month, the sixth year of Bunji era. The end of his life, not at all different from his actions in his earlier time, is to be celebrated. People said to one another that his passing thus is a rare thing in the world of End Times. I wrote to Reverend Jakuren, attaching En'i's poems that I continued to admire.

> Can you imagine a world
> after he uttered
> such fragrant words
> before departing—
> "the middle of spring."

Jien was suggesting that in the dark, degraded age of declined dharma, marked by battles, crimes, fire, and famine, Saigyō's exquisitely timed *nirvāna* radiated a brilliant light.

SAIGYŌ IN THE HISTORY OF JAPANESE LITERATURE

Saigyō had a monk friend named Myōe who was fifty-five years younger. Myōe later became an esteemed practitioner-scholar of the Avatamsaka (Flower Splendor) School of Buddhism, one of the six schools founded in the Nara period (710–794). He was a believer in the traditional elite practice of reciting complex mantras and a fierce critic of Bishop Genshin's simplified chanting of the Pure Land practice for all people. He quoted Saigyō's words:

Waka is the true form of the Tathāgata (Buddha). There-
fore, writing one poem is an intention of carving an im-
age of the Buddha. To keep the mind on one phrase is
no other than chanting an esoteric mantra.

Saigyō was a practitioner of the Shingon School but never
sought to be a high priest. Instead, his pursuit of straightforward
poetic expression was in harmony with his search for dharma.

Dharma Emperor Gotoba, who started his dictatorship as a
retired emperor soon after Saigyō's death, said,

Saigyō is splendid and, further, his heart is particularly
deep and moving. Tendencies that are rare and hard to
come by are both visible in his work. He seems to be
a born poet. Thus, his poems are not to be imitated by
those who are vague-minded. He is a matchless master
impossible to speak about.

Gotoba, who was an outstanding poet himself, ordered a
compilation of *Shinkokin Waka Shū* (*New Ancient and Present Waka
Collection*) in 1201, eleven years after Saigyō's death. There were
six editors, including Sadaie Fujiwara, but Gotoba himself was
passionately engaged in making the selections.

The plan was first to include poems from *Man'yo Shū* (*Ten
Thousand Leaves Collection*), the earliest and largest collection of
Japanese poems, compiled between 759 and 780 in the Nara
period. *Tanka*, or short poems, although one of several differ-
ent types included in the collection, accounted for the majority
of the poems. In the Heian period, however, *tanka* were the ex-

clusively composed Japanese style of poetry, and the commonly used term *waka* (meaning Japanese poems) became synonymous with *tanka*.

Gotoba's *Shinkokin Waka Shū* (New Ancient and Present Waka Collection) also included poems from *Kokin Waka Shū* (*Ancient and Present Waka Collection*), the first imperial anthology, and is regarded as a classical standard published in 905. Gotoba's anthology included poems from the six imperial anthologies that followed *Kokin Waka Shū*. The new collection roughly alternated ancient poets' works with contemporary poems. After going through stages of editing, the *Shinkokin Waka Shū* was finished around 1216. It contains 1,978 poems, making it the largest of the eight imperial anthologies to this point.

During this time of the royal court's declining glory, Sadaie Fujiwara's aesthetics became an essential basis for selecting poems. He followed his father Toshinari's concepts of *yūgen* (elegant, subtle, mysterious, and profound beauty) and *ushin* (heartful, melancholy, and deep feelings). Sadaie himself developed his own poetic term, *yojō yūen no tai*, meaning to embody lingering fascination. Thus, the *Shinkokin Shū* came to be recognized as the ultimate *waka* collection with a highly elaborate and imaginative style, distinct from *Man'yo Shū* and *Kokin Waka Shū*.

Gotoba tried to defeat the new Hōjō warrior clan, against the strong advice of Priest Jien. Gotoba, however, was vanquished and exiled to Oki Island in the Japan Sea in 1221, spending nineteen years there. In the last years of his life, Gotoba removed about four hundred poems from *Shinkokin Waka Shū* and called the resulting shorter version "the authentic *Shinkokin* collection." It is also called the Oki version.

Saigyō's poems were natural, genuine, and contemplative. Bare and defenseless in nature, he touched on the existential loneliness of human beings. Although Saigyō's style was different from Sadaie's artificial and fictional tendency to employ double and triple meanings, Sadaie respected his works highly. Consequently, Saigyō had the most poems in the book at ninety-four; his student Jien followed at ninety-two. It is noteworthy that Saigyō's writing surpassed that of all the royal courtiers, aristocrats, and famed literary figures of Japanese history and that he was regarded as the premier poet in this all-star lineup.

His literary renown endured for centuries. Five hundred years after Saigyō's death, Bashō Matsuo, the legendary haiku poet, wrote in his travel journal *Oi no Kobumi* (*A Short Essay with a Creel*),

In Saigyō's *waka* poems, in Sōgi's linked verse, in Sesshū's painting, in Rikyū's tea, what penetrates is one. Those who live with elegance follow what is created and make the four seasons friends. Where they look, there is nothing but flowers. Where they think, there is nothing but the moon.

Bashō followed in the footsteps of Saigyō and wrote *Oku no Hosomichi* (*Narrow Road to the North*), his renowned travelogue of prose and haiku, at times mentioning Saigyō. Throughout his poetic career, Bashō expressed tremendous reverence for him.

For Saigyō, a genuine relationship with nature came from living in nature, having union with nature, and being nature. This perhaps separates Saigyō from most of his preceding and contemporary court poets, whose poems came from imagining nature and who were often dependent on wit and technical prowess. In one poem Saigyō says,

> From now on let me say
> to those who wish
> to see cherry blossoms—
> renounce the world
> and live in the mountains.

Bashō was one of those who took Saigyō's recommendation seriously, lived in nature, and made deep observations. He became one of Japan's most beloved poets in his own right, renowned for his aesthetics of stillness; serenity; and appreciation of solitude, aging, and decline.

AFTER SAIGYŌ

As far as we know, Saigyō did not write any essays. All he left behind were collections of *waka* poems. Dozens of his *waka* were preceded by headnotes. Although some of them can be dated, it is up to us to guess when the majority of them were written.

Stories about Saigyō appear in essays and story collections created during his life and later. About sixty years after his death, a fictional biography of his dharma-seeking and poetic life emerged—*Saigyō Monogatari* (*Saigyō Stories*), written by an unknown author. It contains 128 poems by Saigyō as well as replies by others. Depicting him as an enlightened practitioner of the Pure Land faith, this book shaped the general perception of Saigyō's life from then on.

The last five years of Saigyō's life (1185–1190) coincided with the beginning of the warrior regime of the Minamoto clan in Kamakura. Around 1224, the military regime led by a *shikken* or regent (instead of a *shōgun*) switched allegiance to the Hōjō clan, starting with Tokimune, which was also based in Kamakura.

In the meantime, during the thirteenth century, new types of Buddhism emerged: the Pure Land School established by Hōnen (1133–1212), the Pure Land True School founded by Shinran (1173–1262), and the Nichiren School by Nichiren (1222–1282). Additionally, Eisai (1141–1215) and Dōgen (1200–1253) went to Song dynasty China and brought back Zen (*Chan* in Chinese) teachings. These two pioneers are regarded as founders of the Rinzai and Soto schools, respectively. Masters of all these new schools emphasized single-hearted practices, either chanting Amitābha Buddha's name, chanting the title of the Lotus Sūtra, or meditating. Moving away from the complex theories and rituals of the traditional Tendai and Shingon schools, such repetition of straightforward practices in the reformed Buddhist schools attracted a majority of Japanese people during the Kamakura period.

Then, in 1336, the Ashikaga clan took power and in 1371 established its administration on Muromachi Street in Kyōto, launching the Muromachi period. The *shōguns* of the Ashikaga clan supported the Rinzai School of Zen and opened major Zen monasteries in Kyōto called the Five Mountains. Thus, the *shōguns* were instrumental in establishing Zen culture with monastic architecture, landscape design, tea ceremony, calligraphy, and Chinese-style poems instead of *waka*.

Saigyō, however, was not forgotten.

In Noh Plays

In this era, Kan'ami (Kiyotsugu Kanze, 1333–1384) created the Noh theater, a form of drama in which there are four main categories of performers: the protagonist, the supporting actor, companions, and musicians. Kan'ami based Noh on *sarugaku* ("monkey music"), a folk theater that incorporated flutes, drums, and song repertoires with a variety of dances from Shintō ceremonies. He took inspiration from classical stories and developed his own scripts.

Kan'ami's company traveled with his young, beautiful actor son Motokiyo (to be called Zeami, 1363?–1443). Yoshimitsu Ashikaga (1358–1408), the third *shōgun* of the Muromachi government, who had built up great wealth by trading with China, loved Motokiyo and the company, and so he made it his official troop.

Kan'ami's play *Eguchi*, based on Saigyō's *waka* exchange with a prostitute in Eguchi, is likely one of the earliest pieces among Saigyō-related Noh plays. The first protagonist (*mae shite*) plays the role of a village woman, actually the spirit of the prostitute. The second protagonist (*ato shite*) represents her ghost. The companions (*tsure*) are her two maids. The supporting actor (*waki*) is a pilgrim. His companions are two monks traveling with him. Another, a local man, provides a form of comic relief typically found in Kyōgen plays, which are part of the Noh theater but have more emphasis on laughter. The drama goes as follows: When a group of traveling monks hum Saigyō's poem at the tomb of the prostitute, a village woman asks them why they are not chanting the courtesan's reply. She recites her poem and confesses that she is the spirit of the woman and disappears. That night the prostitute and her attendants appear riding on a boat. She dances in the moonlight while singing about the impermanence of the world and the suffering of her life, having to sell her body. After stating that all comes from delusion, she turns herself into Samantabhadra Bodhisattva. The boat is transformed into an elephant, and a white cloud appears. The bodhisattva gets on the cloud and disappears into the western sky.

After Kan'ami's death, Zeami took over the company and further established the Noh theater and its dramaturgy as the author of *Fūshi Kaden* (*Shape of Wind, Transmission of Flower*) and *Kakyō* (*Flower Mirror*). Zeami adopted Toshinari Fujiwara's concept of *yūgen*—an aesthetic of elegant, subtle, mysterious, and profound beauty—as the ideal overtone of high theater.

Ugetsu (*Rain and Moon*), written by Zeami, presents a secondary actor who performs the role of Saigyō. The main actor is an old man, and his companion is an old woman. First, Saigyō introduces himself and says that he is on his way to visit Sumitomo Shrine in Settsu Province (present-day Ōsaka Prefecture), having arrived in the region while night is drawing near. So he goes to a humble hut, wanting to ask for lodging. There he finds an old couple arguing. The woman likes moonlight leaking into the hut, so she doesn't want the roof fixed. The man likes to listen to the sound of rain, so he wants the roof in good shape. He says, "We take the trouble to thatch these humble eaves." Thinking these words can be used as the last half of a poem, he says to Saigyō, "If you complete this poem, we will let you stay in our house." Saigyō answers, "The moon leaks, rain forms puddles, and yet . . ." The couple is impressed and lets him stay. At night, the god Sumiyoshi, performed by the second main actor, appears in Saigyō's dream. The old man turns out to be a Shintō priest who prays and dances.

Sanekata, also by Zeami, is based on the story of Sanekata Fujiwara (?–999), a poet who served the emperor and was then demoted to governor of the far northern Mutsu Province, where he died. One of the lead actors plays the role of old Sanekata, and the other enacts his spirit. The supporting actor is Saigyō, and the comic actor plays a villager. In the play, Saigyō travels to Mutsu and is told by a villager that one of the tombs is that of Sanekata. When Saigyō offers a poem, an old Sanekata appears, asks Saigyō if the *Shinkokin Waka Shū* has been completed, and talks about ancient poems. Then he announces that he will dance in a festival in Kyōto and flies away. That night in Saigyō's dream, the spirit of Sanekata appears and talks about his own past glory. The spirit looks at his reflection in the water in a basin and is shocked and disgusted by his aged appearance. He disappears when thunder roars.

The number of Noh plays related to Saigyō is illustrative of his impact on Japanese culture—he is featured in more plays than any other poet or historical figure. He serves as the protagonist in *Saigyō Zuka* (*Saigyō Tomb*) and as a supporting role in such plays as *Hatsuse Saigyō* (*Saigyō at Mount Hatsue*); *Genzai Eguchi* (*Present-day Eguchi*); *Ume Hama* (Ume Beach); *Saigyō Saijū* (*Saigyō and Saijū*); and *Matsuyama Tengu* (*Long-nosed Goblin of Matsuyama*), also called *Sutoku*. Saigyō's name is not mentioned in *Akogi* (*Akogi Bay*), but the old man's spirit reflecting on a one-time love affair with a noble lady is commonly understood to be Saigyō's voice. The reason for his recurring appearance in Noh theater may be that Saigyō's poems address recently deceased or historical poets as if they are alive and treat natural objects, such as trees and wind, just like human beings—literary devices that Noh theater also utilizes.

Yugyō Yanagi (*Traveling Sage and the Willow*) is a large and still widely performed piece, written by Kojirō Kanze (1435–1516). It is based on Saigyō's *waka*, which was included in the *Shinkokin Waka Shū*. One of the lead actors performs the role of an old villager. The other enacts the spirit of a willow tree. The subordinate role is that of an itinerant priest who teaches how to chant the Buddha's name. The comic actor plays a villager. The plot follows a traveling monk, who, after passing the Shirakawa Barrier in Mutsu Province, is addressed by an old man and guided to a famous "decayed willow tree." When the monk asks the origin of the name, the old man explains that this is the tree Reverend Saigyō wrote about:

> By the side of the road,
> clear water flows
> in the shade of a willow—
> I stop here to stand
> just a moment.

The old man receives ten recitations of the Buddha's name from the mendicant and disappears into the shade of the tree. That night, while the mendicant keeps chanting, the white-haired spirit of the tree appears and says that even grass and trees can be enlightened owing to the merit of the monk's recitation and Saigyō's *waka*. The spirit dances in gratitude and disappears at dawn.

Saigyō Zakura (*Saigyō's Cherry Blossoms*), written by Zeami, is the most famous of all Saigyō-related Noh, appealing to the later Japanese obsession with blooming cherry blossoms. The protagonist is the spirit of an old cherry tree. The secondary role is Saigyō. The companions represent several viewers of cherry blossoms, and the comic actor plays Saigyō's attendant novice. In the play, Saigyō lives in a hut in Saga. He is looking forward to quietly enjoying the cherry blossoms and calls his attendant to ask him not to let in visitors. But a group of men comes from afar who enthusiastically beg to see the cherry blossoms, so Saigyō unwillingly admits them. Thinking that he has abandoned worldly affairs only to find himself right in the middle of them, he sighs and chants,

> People keep flocking
> in groups
> to view the flowers—
> regrettably,
> the cherry blossoms are to blame!

The visitors forget about going home and lie down under the tree; so does Saigyō. That night the spirit of the old cherry tree appears in Saigyō's dream. It resents his remark about "the fault of cherry blossoms" and insists that cherry blossoms just bloom with no mind and are not at fault; it is Saigyō's choice of perception as to whether he is in a worldly place or a place of retreat. The spirit suggests that blossoms that bloom in time are an expression of buddha dharma. It goes on to describe blooming flowers in noted sites and speaks of the glory of life. At dawn the spirit bids him farewell and disappears. Saigyō wakes up covered with fallen petals.

These plays are all excellent examples of how Saigyō's body of work helped shape Japan's artistic culture—a culture that appreciates the power of poetry and identifies with the beauty of the natural world.

—KAZUAKI TANAHASHI

Notes to the Reader

Dates

This book follows the lunar calendar of twenty-eight days used traditionally in East Asia. The first to third months correspond to spring, and the other seasons follow in three-month periods. The fifteenth day of the month is the day of the full moon. (An extra month is occasionally added to make up a year.)

Age

This book follows the traditional East Asian way of counting ages, wherein a person is one year old at birth and gains a year on New Year's Day.

Presentation

On each page of the main part of this book, we present our translation of a poem, complete with Saigyō's original title and/or headnote where applicable. The translation is followed by the Japanese pronunciation—with slashes indicating breaks in the phrasing—and the text in Japanese.

Pronunciation and Syllables

In the romanization of Japanese words, a vowel is always pronounced without change regardless of another vowel before or after.

A macron, e.g., ō, indicates a long vowel. In this book, macrons are not used in the bibliography.

The phonetic (*hiragana*) letter は (*ha*) is sometimes pronounced *wa*.

The consonant *n* forms an independent syllable. The apostrophe after *n* means it does not link with the following vowel; i.e., the *n* and *a* in *n'a* are pronounced separately instead of as *na*.

PHONETIC LETTERS AND IDEOGRAPHS

Most Japanese words can be written in either phonetic letters or ideographs (*kanji*). *Waka* poems in Saigyō's time were largely written in phonetic letters, in some cases with a small number of ideographs. However, it is customary today to print poems with a higher proportion of ideographs to clarify the meanings. We follow this convention.

In this book, the unabbreviated forms of ideographs are used.

NOTES

An asterisk (*) with the poem number indicates that there is a note to the poem in the back matter of this book.

POEMS

RENUNCIATION

Renunciation means to become a monk, which Saigyō did when he ordained at twenty-three years old. It shaped his life and poetry. Such a deed is also characterized as leaving the household (*shukke*, 出家), escaping from the world (*tonsei*, 遁世), or casting off the world (*yosute*, 世捨て). For Saigyō to remain a samurai meant following a strict social norm, receiving orders from the emperor or others, and having no choice but to fight in times of war. Rather than follow that way of life, he decided to free himself from those obligations and the potential for violence and to express his freedom and spiritual aspiration by begging for food, wandering the countryside, and being true to himself. Of course, his chosen path was not easy, but it was entirely his.

Since my heart
stays attached
to things—
I grow more weary
of the world.

*Nanigoto ni / tomaru kokoro no / ari kere ba /
sarani shi mo mata/ yo no itowashi ki*

何事に留まる心の有りければ更にしも又世の厭はしき

Today's world
is a boat
with no place to anchor—
neither flowing on waves,
nor leaving the shore.

Tomari naki / konogoro no yo wa / fune nare ya /
nami ni mo tsuka zu / iso mo hanare nu

泊りなき此頃の世は舟なれや波にも付かず磯も離れぬ

3*

Written upon leaving the household and bidding fare-
well to Former Emperor Toba.

Though I hold this world
dear, I cannot remain
attached—
only by forsaking the self
can I be free.

*Oshimu tote / oshima re nu beki / kono yo ka wa /
mi wo sute te koso / mi wo mo tasuke me*

惜しむとて惜しまれぬべき此世かは身を捨ててこそ身をも助けめ

4*

If you keep flowing in the three realms, you cannot be free from obligations and love. If you run from obligations and enter not-doing, you can truly return favors to those who have been kind to you.

> My own thinking
> is difficult to abandon,
> still, I will cast it off
> and leave—
> the true way must be true.

Sute gataki / omoi nare domo / sute te ide mu /
makoto no michi zo / makoto naru beki

捨て難き思ひなれども捨てて山でむ眞の道ぞ眞なるべき

When I was on my way to the Tennō Temple, it rained. I asked for shelter at a house in the pleasure quarter called Eguchi, but I was turned away. So I wrote this:

> To abandon the world
> one must be firm—
> but you must be just as certain,
> not sharing this shelter
> for a little while.

*Yononaka wo / itou made koso / katakara me /
kari no yadori wo / oshimu kimi kana*

世の中を厭ふまでこそ堅からめ仮の宿りを惜しむ君哉

6

A reply by the woman at Eguchi:

Hearing you are
a home leaver—
I hope
you're not attached
to this temporary abode!

Ie wo izuru / hito to shi kike ba / kari no yado ni /
kokoro tomu na to / omou bakari zo

家を出づる人とし聞けば仮りの宿に心留むなと思ふ許りぞ

Renouncing the world, I was living in Kurama, north
of Kyōto, at the foot of Mount Hiei. The bamboo con-
duit was frozen, and water stopped coming through.
Hearing that it would be like this until spring, I wrote:

> It makes no sense,
> I thought I'd given up everything—
> now that water is frozen
> in the bamboo pipe,
> I long for spring.

*Wari nashi ya / kōru kakehi no / mizu yue ni /
omoi sute te shi / haru no mata ruru*

理なしや氷る懸樋の水故に思ひ捨ててし春の待たるる

8

How can my heart
still be drenched
with the color of these flowers?
I thought
I had abandoned everything.

Hana ni somu / kokoro no ikade / nokori ke n /
sutehate te ki to / omou waga mi ni

花に染む心の如何で残りけん捨て果てきと思ふ我身に

9

Do those who
renounce the self,
truly renounce?
Not renouncing
is, indeed, renouncing!

*Mi wo sutsuru / hito wa makotoni / sutsuru ka wa /
sute nu hito koso / sutsuru nari keri*

身を捨つる人は眞に捨つるかは捨てぬ人こそ捨つるなりけり

I would have ended up
never realizing
my misfortune—
if there was no way
to renounce this world.

*Mi no usa wo omoi shira de ya / yami na mashi /
somuku narai no / naki yo nari se ba*

身の憂さを思ひ知らで罷みなまし背く慣ひの無き世なりせば

11*

At Mount Suzuka, on my way to Ise Province after re-
nouncing the world:

> Mount Suzuka,
> since I've cast away
> this floating world—
> what will become
> of my life?

Suzuka Yama / ukiyo wo yoso ni / furisute te /
ikani nariyuku / waga mi naru ran

鈴鹿山憂き世をよそに振り捨てていかになり行くわが身なるらん

12

From now on let me say
to those who wish
to see cherry blossoms—
renounce the world
and live in the mountains.

Ima yoro wa / hana mi n hito ni / tsutae oka n /
yo wo nogare tsutsu / yama ni sumae to

今よりは花見ん人に伝へおかん世を遁れつつ山に住まへと

13

If in the next life
we could see
such a moon—
no one would cling
to this one.

Ko n yo ni mo / kakaru tsuki wo shi / miru beku wa /
inochi wo oshimu / hito nakara mashi

来ん世にも斯かる月をし見るべくは命を惜しむ人無からまし

MOON

The lunar calendar used in Japan until modern times, when the solar calendar replaced it, was based on a style that originally came from China. It starts with the day of a new moon, and the fifteenth day of each month represents the day of the full moon, which in Buddhism symbolizes enlightenment. Under this calendar system, the moon dominates people's feelings, consciousness, aesthetics, and schedules.

In Japanese, *tsuki* (月) means "moon" as well as "month." *Tsuki kage* (月影) means "moonlight." The word *kage* has a wide range of meanings, including "shadow," "shade," "shelter," "image," and "light"—anything dark or light created by sunlight.

In Saigyō's poetry, the moon is an ideal that symbolizes clarity, love, memory, and dreams.

14

Just think of the moonlight—
it even shines
on the furthest edge
of an unseen
ordinary mountain.

Hito mo mi nu / yoshi naki yama no / sue made ni /
sumu ran tsuki no / kage wo koso omoe

人も見ぬ由なき山の末までに澄むらん月の影をこそ思へ

15

Cupped in my hands,
the moon reflects
in clear water—
it's not a mirror
I can hold.

*Musumi aguru / izumi ni sume ru / tsukikage wa /
te ni mo tora re nu / kagami nari keri*

掬び上ぐる泉に澄める月影は手にも取られぬ鏡なりけり

16

Not a cloud,
but it looks hazy
ringed
by mist—
this evening moon in spring.

*Kumo nara de / oboro nari to mo / miyuru kana /
kasumi kakare ru / haru no yo no tsuki*

雲ならで朧なりとも見ゆるかな霞掛れる春の夜の月

17

Summer Moon

After the evening shower,
the moon abides
on a floating lotus leaf—
jewels
scatter and sway.

*Yūdachi no / harure ba tsuki zo / yadori keru / tama yuri sufuru /
hasu no ukiha ni*

夕立の晴るれば月ぞ宿りける玉揺り据ふる蓮の浮葉に

18

Wind blowing down
from the mountain
covers the moon with leaves—
shadows mingled
with light.

Yamaoroshi no / tsuki ni konoha wo / fukikake te /
hikari ni magau / kage wo miru kana

山嵐の月に木の葉を吹き掛けて光に紛ふ影を見るかな哉

19

I waited to go out
until I saw this evening's
clear moon—
a cloud
suddenly covers my heart.

Machi ide te / kuma naki yoi no / tsuki mire ba /
kumo zo kokoro ni / mazu kakari keru

待ち出でて隈なき宵の月見れば雲ぞ心に先づ掛りける

Should I dye
my heart
the pure color of the moon—
while I'm not leaving
the capital?

Tsuki no iro ni / kokoro wo kiyoku / some mashi ya /
miyako wo ide nu / waga mi nari se ba

月の色に心を清く染めましや都を出でぬ我が身なりせば

If only someone
knew how I feel
when the moon appears at dawn—
I would not blame myself
forever.

Omoi shiru / hito ariake no / yo nari se ba /
tsuki se zu mi wo ba / urami zara mashi

思ひ知る人有明の世なりせば尽きせず身をば恨みざらまし

22[*]

Leaves have fallen
in the village
at the foot of Mount Ogura—
looking through branches,
now I can see the moon.

Ogura Yama / fumoto no sato ni / konoha chire ba /
kozue ni haruru / tsuki wo miru kana

小倉山麓の里に木の葉ちれば梢に晴るゝ月を見る哉

23

If this were a world
where flowers never fell
and clouds
didn't hide the moon—
I wouldn't worry about a thing.

Hana chira de / tsuki wa kumora nu / yo nari se ba /
mono wo omowa nu / waga mi nara mashi

花散らで月は曇らぬ世なりせば物を思はぬ我身ならまし

24

A feeling
beyond compare
this autumn night—
beneath a pristine moon,
the cry of a buck.

Tagui naki / kokochi koso sure / aki no yo no /
tsuki sumu mine no / saoshika no koe

類なき心地こそすれ秋の夜の月澄む峰の小牡鹿の声

25*

Everything in the heavens
comes out
through the same cave door—
but the light is different
this autumn moon.

*Ama no hara / onaji iwato wo / izure domo /
hikari kotonaru / aki no yo no tsuki*

天の原同じ岩戸を出づれども光異なる秋の夜の月

26

All night long
moonlight
lingers on my sleeve—
I reflect on autumns
in the past.

Yomosuraga / tsuki koso sode ni / yadori kere /
mukashi no aki wo / omoi izure ba

夜もすがら月こそ袖に宿りけれ昔の秋を思ひ出づれば

Gazing at the moon
lightened my heart
in a former time—
now I meet it
once again.

*Tsuki wo mi te / kokoro ukare shi / inishie no /
aki ni mo sarani / meguriai nuru*

月を見て心浮かれし古への秋にも更に巡り逢ひぬる

28

Moonlight spills
onto my sleeve—
in this tumbledown
grass hut,
I can only gaze.

Abaretaru / kusa no iori ni / moru tsuki wo /
sode ni utsushi te / nagame tsuru kana

荒れたる草の庵に洩る月を袖に移して眺めつるかな

Viewing the Moon through the Night

While I wondered
who the moonlight
might tempt to come by—
night turned
into dawn.

Tare ki na n / tsuki no hikari ni / sasowa re te /
to omou ni yowa no / ake nu naru kana

誰来なん月の光に誘はれてと思ふに夜半の明けぬ成る哉

MOUNTAIN ABODE

Saigyō called the largest collection of his own poems *Sanka Shū* (山家集), meaning *Mountain Abode Collection* or *Mountain Home Anthology*. It is a summary of his life.

What Saigyō calls "home" must have been a shack with thin walls and a thatched roof, perhaps ten feet square. There was little division between the inside dwelling area and the natural world outside. No neighbors, no stores, no merchants, no traffic, and no human noise. He dwelled right in the midst of sunshine, moonlight, wind, rain, snow, quietude, and birdsong. He was in nature, and he was nature.

In springtime,
you became my friend
at the hermitage—
please don't leave your old nest,
valley nightingale.

Haru no hodo wa / wa ga sumu io no / tomo ni nari te /
furusu na ide so / tani no uguisu

春の程は我が住む庵の友に成て古巣な出でそ谷の鶯

Close to my hut
on a hilly rice field,
I was startled
by the voice of a deer—
then I surprised the deer!

*Oyamada no / io chikaku / naku shika no /
ne ni odorokasa re te / odorokasu kana*

小山田の庵近く鳴く鹿の音に驚かされて驚かす哉

32

At my hermitage
I planted
an orange mandarin—
I'll wait here,
until the mountain cuckoo comes.

Waga yado ni / hana tachibana wo / ue te koso /
yama hototogisu / matsu bekari kere

我宿に花橘を植ゑてこそ山杜鵑待つべかりけれ

33[*]

The moon leaks in,
rains form puddles—
still, we take the trouble
to thatch
these humble eaves.

*Tsuki wa more / ame wa tamare do / tonikakuni /
shizu ga nokiba wo / fuki zo wazurau*

月は漏れ雨は溜まれど兎に角に賤が軒端を葺きぞ煩ふ

It's the sound of bamboo,
above all,
as I rest on my pillow—
together with
windblown hail.

Take no ne no / waki te makura ni / sayuru kana /
kaze ni arare no / guse rare ni keri

竹の音の分きて枕に冴ゆるかな風に霰の具せられにけり

35

Who could bear
the desolation
of a mountain village—
fierce rains fall
from the evening sky.

*Tare sumi te / aware wo shiru ran / yamazato no /
ame furi susamu / yūgure no sora*

誰住みて哀れ知るらん山里の雨降り荒む夕暮の空

Leaves bury
the path
to this hut—
my winter seclusion
so soon!

Michi mo nashi / yado wa konoha ni / uzumore te /
madaki se sasuru / fuyugomori kana

道も無し宿は木の葉に埋もれて夙き為さする冬籠り哉

37

Creepers wither
in the mountain village,
I slip open the bamboo door—
again, mounds of deep snow
block my path.

Mugura kare te / take no to akuru / yamazato ni /
mata michi tozuru / yuki tsumoru meri

葎枯れて竹の戸開くる山里に又道閉づる雪積るめり

38

No one will visit
my hut
by the end of the year—
deep snow
on the mountain path.

Toshi no uchi wa / tou hito sarani / ara ji kashi /
yuki mo yamaji mo / fukaki sumika wo

年の内は訪ふ人更に有らじかし雪も山路も深き栖を

39

My hope to have someone visit
has disappeared—
if I didn't enjoy
this mountain village solitude,
it would be painful to live.

*Tou hito no / omoi tae taru / yamazato no /
sabishisa naku wa / sumiukara mashi*

訪ふ人も思ひ絶えたる山里の淋しさ無くは住み憂からまし

Putting in
a newly knit
brushwood door—
I pass my time
waiting for the new year to come.

Atarashiki / shiba no amido wo / tatekae te /
toshi no akuru wo / machi wataru kana

新しき柴の編み戸を立て換えて年の明くるを待ち渡る哉

While sleeping,
I thought last year had ended
and this year arrived—
my first dream of the year
came true!

Toshi kure nu / haru ku beshi to wa / omoi ne ni /
masashiku mie te / kanau hatsuyume

年暮れぬ春来べしとは思ひ寝に正しく見えて叶ふ初夢

42

MIST AROUND MY MOUNTAIN ABODE

Outside the thatched bamboo door
a thick fog
spreads through the night—
if it clears off
daybreak may come soon.

*Yo wo kome te / take no amido ni / tatsu kiri no /
hare ba yagate ya / ake n to su ran*

夜を籠めて竹の編み戸に立つ霧の晴れば軈てや明けんとすらん

43

Without expecting it,
today
I will return home—
after picking young herbs
in a snowy field.

Kyō wa tada / omoi mo yora de / kaeri namu /
yuki tsumu nobe no / wakaba nari keri

今日は唯思ひも寄らで帰りなむ雪つむ野辺の若葉なりけり

44

Please come—
the plum blossoms are in full bloom.
Though I rarely see you,
I hope you'll visit my hut
from time to time.

Tomeko kashi / mume sakarinaru / waga yado wo /
utoki mo hito wa / orini koso yore

尋め来かし梅盛りなる我宿を疎きも人は折にこそ寄れ

JOURNEY

In ancient Japan, most people were bound to their lands, workplaces, and homes; they rarely traveled far, except for journeys to important Shintō shrines and Buddhist temples for worship. On the other hand, as a wandering monk, Saigyō was free to visit famous sites of poetry and beautiful scenery. He was safe in his travels since he had no possessions. There were always temples where he could stay, and he begged for food wherever he was able. Without a map, he must have become lost many times, and since he did not necessarily understand local dialects, from time to time he may have struggled to communicate. There was also no assurance that people would be hospitable to a tired, shabby, traveling monk.

45

The sound of the bell,
a storm
at dawn—
hearing it deeply
my heart replies.

Akatsuki no / arashi ni taguu / kane no ne wo /
kokoro no soko ni / kotaete zo kiku

暁の嵐に類う鐘の音を心の底に答へてぞ聞

46

Ice locked between rocks
begins to melt
this morning—
perhaps water beneath the moss
is seeking its path.

Iwama toji shi / kōri mo kesa wa / tokesome te /
koke no shitamitzu / michi motomu ran

岩間閉し氷も今朝は溶け初めて苔の下水道求むらん

47

Tender maid blossoms
withered
by nighttime dew,
awaken to play
in the moonlit dawn.

Yoi no ma no / tsuyu ni shiore te / ominaeshi /
ariake no tsuki no / kage ni tawaru ru

宵の間の露に萎れて女郎花有明の月の影に戯るる

48

Longing for the one
I left behind,
I make my way through—
the sleeves of my robe
pushed back by bushes in dew.

Omoi oku / hito no kokoro ni / shitawa re te /
tsuyu wakuru sode no / kaeri nuru kana

思ひ置く人の心に慕はれて露分くる袖の返りぬる哉

49

Though not a pair,
its reflection
is its companion—
a mandarin duck
living at a mountain stream.

*Tsugawa ne do / utsure ba kage wo / tomo to shi te /
oshi sumi keri na / yamakawa no mizu*

番はねど映れば影を友として鴛鴦棲みけりな山川の水

50

Without marking my way back
with broken branches,
I want to go deeply into the mountain—
is there a place
where misery isn't heard?

Shiori se de / nao yama fukaku / wake ira n /
uki koto kika nu / tokoro ari ya to

枝折せで猶山深く分け入らん憂き事聞かぬ所有りやと

Listening to Insects Alone

Lying in bed alone,
I hear the chirp
of grasshoppers—
since they're not my companions,
my brooding grows.

Hitorine no / tomo ni wa nara de / kirigirisu /
naku ne wo kike ba / mono omoi sou

一人寝の友にはならで蟋斯鳴く音を聞けば物思添ふ

EARLY AUTUMN

Since the wind carries
so many tender feelings
through the treetops—
I know it is autumn
in this deep mountain village.

Samazama no / aware wo kome te / kozue fuku /
kaze ni aki shiru / miyamabe no sato

様々の哀れをこめて梢吹く風に秋知る深山辺の里

53*

Sleeping by myself
in the evening chill,
I want to add
another layer—
for whom is she pounding a robe?

*Hitorine no / yosamu ni naru ni / kasane baya /
ta ga tame ni utsu / koromo naru ran*

一人寝の夜寒になるに重ねばや誰がために打つ衣なるらん

54

Beneath the weeds,
grasshoppers
are buried in frost—
I can just make out
their song.

*Shimo uzumu / mugura ga shita no / kirigirisu /
aru ka naki ka no / koe kikoyu nari*

霜埋む葎が下の蟋有るか無きかの声聞ゆなり

55

When snow falls,
burying the paths
of mountains and fields,
beneath the sky of my journey
I can't tell here from there.

Yuku fure ba / noji mo yamaji mo / uzumore te /
ochikochi shira nu / tabi no sora kana

雪降れば野路も山路も埋もれて遠近知らぬ旅の空かな

56

Since I'm not in a hurry,
stopped by snow—
I'll wait
in this mountain village
until spring.

*Isoga zu wa / yuki ni waga mi ya / tome rare te /
yamabe no sato ni / haru wo mata mashi*

急がずは雪に我身や止られて山辺の里に春を待たまし

57

I feel more
forlorn
than usual—
traveling in a strange land
at the end of the year.

Tsune yorimo / kokorobosoku zo / omooyu ru /
tabi no sora nite / toshi no kure nuru

常よりも心細くぞ思ほゆる旅の空にて年の暮れぬる

58*

Written on visiting the eastern provinces:

After so many years,
how could I have imagined?
What a life!
Once again crossing
the middle mountains of Saya.

Toshi take te / mata koyu beshi to / omoi ki ya /
inochi nari keri / Sayo no Nakayama

年長けて又越ゆべしと思ひきや命なりけり佐夜の中山

FALLING PETALS

In my travels,
I slept beneath a tree
on Mount Yoshino—
the spring wind covered me
with a quilt of flowers.

Ko no moto ni / tabine wo sure ba / Yoshino Yama /
hana no fusuma wo / kisuru harukaze

木の本に旅寝をすれば吉野山花の襖を着する春風

REFLECTION

In the stream bed,
a deep green color
can be seen—
waves ripple in the wind,
river willow.

Minasoko ni / fukaki midori no / iro mie te /
kaze ni nami yoru / kawayanagi kana

水底に深き緑の色見えて風に波寄る川柳かな

61

Announcing spring,
a valley brook
trickles from ice
between boulders—
its time for resting over.

Haru shire to / tani no hosomizu / mori zo kuru /
iwama no kōri / hima tae ni keri

春知れと谷の細水洩りぞくる岩間の氷暇絶えにけり

BLOSSOM AWAKENINGS

In *waka* poetry, *hana* ("flowers") without any particular specification usually means cherry blossoms. They bloom gorgeously in midspring for several days, and then they start to fall. Their fleeting beauty is characterized as *aware*, the principal concept of this genre of poetry.

Aware can be written as 哀れ, which emphasizes "pathos," "misery," and "pity." It can also be written with phonetic letters alone as あはれ (classical) or あわれ (modern), which indicates a broader meaning such as "deep feeling," "melancholy," "splendid," and "sublime." The word suggests "beautiful to the point of sadness." Thus, *aware* expresses not only one's feelings but an awakening to the reality of nature's depth.

62*

How I wish
I could die
beneath cherry blossoms—
in the middle of spring
when the moon is full.

Negawaku wa / hana no shita ni te / haru shina n /
sono kisaragi no / mochizuki no koro

願はくは花の下にて春死なんその如月の望月の頃

63

How close to me
the blossoms
must feel—
counting up all the springs
I've come to see them.

Hana ikani / ware wo aware to / omou ramu /
mi te sugi ni keru / haru wo kazoe te

花如何に我を哀れと思ふらむ見て過にける春を数へて

64

Spreading everywhere,
cherry blossoms
are in full bloom—
white clouds drape
the edge of every mountain.

Oshinabe te / hana no sakari ni / nari ni keri /
yama no ha gotoni / kakaru shirakumo

押並べて花の盛りに成にけり 山の端ごとに掛る白雲

65

I wish to remember
floating on waves
of cherry blossoms—
coming down like a waterfall
from a white cloud's peak.

Omoide ni / hana no nami ni mo / nagare baya /
mine no shirakumo / taki kudasu meri

思ひ出でに花の波にも流ればや峰の白雲滝下すめり

66*

Sleeping alone
on my grass pillow,
the fragrance
of plum blossoms
reaches me from the nearby fence.

Hitori nuru / kusa no makura no / utsurika wa /
kakine no mume no / nioi nari keri

一人寝る草の枕の移り香は垣根の梅の匂ひなりけり

67*

While living in Saga, plum blossoms fell around my hut in the wind; they came from someone's abode across the path.

> Why is my neighbor
> so annoyed
> when the wind blows in this direction?
> Plum blossom fragrance
> delights me so.

Nushi ika ni / kaze wataru to te / itou ran /
yoso ni ureshiki / ume no nioi wo

主如何に風渡るとて厭ふらん他所に嬉しき梅の匂ひを

68*

People keep flocking
in groups
to view the flowers—
regrettably,
the cherry blossoms are to blame!

*Hanami ni to / mure tsutsu hito no / kuru nomi zo /
atara sakura no / toga ni wa ari keru*

花見にと群れつつ人の来るのみぞ可惜桜の咎にはありける

69*

In Shirakawa,
a nightingale sings
on a springtime twig—
as if listening
to what the cherry blossoms say.

*Shirakawa no / haru no kozue no / uguisu wa /
hana no kotoba wo / kiku kokochi suru*

白川の春の梢の鶯は花の言葉を聞く心地する

70*

Mount Yoshino—
instead of taking last year's path
marked by broken branches,
I want to call on flowers
I haven't seen.

*Yoshino Yama / kozo no shiori no / michi kae te /
mada mi nu kata no / hana wo tazune n*

吉野山去年の枝折の道変て未だ見ぬ方の花を尋ねん

On Mount Yoshino,
snow scatters
over cherry branches—
this year's blossoms
may be slightly late.

*Yoshino Yama / sakura ga eda ni / yuki chiri te /
hana osogenaru / toshi ni mo aru kana*

吉野山櫻が枝に雪散りて花遅げなる年にも有る哉

VISITING MOUNTAIN FLOWERS ALONE

Who else
would search for cherry blossoms
on Mount Yoshino—
pressing ahead
on mossy rocks?

Tare ka mata / hana wo tazune te / Yoshino Yama /
koke fumi wakuru / iwa tsutau ran

誰か又花を尋ねて吉野山苔踏み分くる岩伝ふらん

73

I no longer think
of leaving Mount Yoshino—
though "after the blossoms fall"
people
may expect me.

Yoshino Yama / yagate ide ji to / omou mi wo /
hana chiri na ba to / hito ya matsu ran

吉野山やがて出でじと思ふ身を花散りなばと人や待つらん

74

Mount Yoshino,
since the day I saw
branches with cherry blossoms
to their tips—
my heart and body have been apart.

Yoshino Yama / kozue no hana wo / mi shi hi yori /
kokoro wa mi ni mo / sowa zu nari ni ki

吉野山梢の花を見し日より心は身にも添はず成にき

75

Scattering the heart of one
who can't bear parting—
the spring mountain breeze
entices
cherry petals away.

Oshimu hito no / kokoro wo sae ni / chirasu kana /
hana wo sasoe ru / haru no yamakaze

惜しむ人の心をさへに散らす哉花を誘へる春の山風

Indeed, my heart floats away
with its love of
mountain cherry blossoms—
will it return to me,
after they fall?

Akugaru ru / kokoro wa satemo / yamazakura /
chiri nan nochi ya / mi ni kaeru beki

憧るる心は扨も山桜散りなん後や身に帰るべき

No one
in this world
would cling to life,
if they thought of themselves
as cherry blossoms that fall.

Inochi oshimu / hito ya kono yo ni / nakara mashi /
hana ni kawari te / chiru mi to omowa ba

命惜しむ人や此の世に無からまし花に代りて散る身と思はば

HEART OF AUTUMN

The season of harvest is not only for farmers and land-owners. Fruits are abundant in the mountains, and mushrooms abound. Leaves, trees, and vines turn brilliant colors, while the moon is particularly clear during this season. But autumn is also the time for decay. Plants begin to wither. The songs of insects become weaker. Temperatures drop, and winds turn fierce.

As autumn deepens, there is often an anticipation of cold, freezes, dark, and misery. One who lives alone becomes more alone. Isolation and sadness increase. There is no assurance that the poet will get through the winter of one long, fearful night after another. *Ah.*

By and large,
even for someone who doesn't
feel things deeply—
autumn's first wind
touches the heart.

Oshinabe te / mono wo omowa nu / hito ni sae /
kokoro wo tsukuru / aki no hatsukaze

押し並べて物を思はぬ人にさえ心を付くる秋の初風

79

It's hard to tell
why—
autumn makes everything
feel oddly
sad.

Obotukana / aki wa ikanaru / yue no are ba /
suzuroni mono no / kanasikaru ran

覚束な秋は如何なる故のあれば漫に物の悲しかるらん

Cloud layers
part in the wind—
at dawn,
the first callings of geese
fly past the mountain.

Yokogumo no / kaze ni wakaru ru / shinonome ni /
yama tobi koyu ru / hatsukari no koe

横雲の風に別るる東雲に山飛び越ゆる初雁の声

Without counting the days,
I know from the face
of this evening's moon
in the sky—
it's the midpoint of autumn.

Kazoe ne do / koyoi no tsuki no / keshiki ni te /
aki no nakaba wo / sora ni shiru kana

数へねど今夜の月の気色にて秋の半ばを空に知る哉

Hearing the songs of insects
grow more faint—
in my heart
I count
the remaining days of autumn.

Mushi no ne wo / yowari yuku ka to / kiku kara ni /
kokoro ni aki no / hikazu wo zo furu

虫の音を弱り行くかと聞くからに心に秋の日数をぞ経る

HOLDING AUTUMN DEAR THROUGH THE NIGHT

Though autumn is dear to me,
even the sound
of the temple bell
is changing—
will dewdrops blend into frost?

Oshime domo / kaze no oto sae / kawaru kana /
shimo ni ya tsuyu wo / musubi kauru ran

惜しめども鐘の音さへ変る哉霜にや露を結び換ふらん

84*

How wondrous!
Dewdrops slipping
from blades of grass—
autumn winds rising
on Miyagino field.

Aware ikani / kusaba no tsuyu no / koboru ran
akikaze tachi nu / Miyagi No no hara

哀れ如何に草葉の露の零るらん秋風立ちぬ宮城野の原

85*

Dwarf bamboo in autumn,
maybe an early winter shower
in the nearby mountain village—
clouds cover
Ikoma Peak.

*Akishino ya / toyama no sato ya / shiguru ran /
Ikoma no take ni / kumo no kakare ru*

秋篠や外山の里や時雨るらん生駒の岳に雲の掛かれる

Spindler leaves entangling the pine
have fallen—
autumn winds
on the outlying mountains
must be fierce.

Matsu ni hau / masa no hakazura / chiri ni keri /
toyama no aki ni / kaze susamu ran

松に這う柾の葉葛散りにけり外山の秋に風荒むらん

It makes all things
sad
in the howling winds,
everywhere ghostly—
autumn dusk.

Fuki watasu / kaze ni aware wo / hitoshime te /
izuku mo sugoki / aki no yūgure

吹き渡す風に哀れを等しめて何処も凄き秋の夕暮

MAPLE LEAVES

Autumn's brocade
covers
the branches—
a distancing mist
turns everything dark.

Nishiki haru / aki no kozue wo / mise nu kana /
hedatsuru kiri no / yami wo tsukuri te

錦張る秋の梢を見せぬ哉隔つる霧の闇を作りて

At the end of autumn, Jakunen visited Mount Kōya.
I express my feeling on the passing of autumn.

The capital city
I knew so well
feels distant now—
my sadness grows
in the autumn dusk.

*Nareki ni shi / miyako mo utoku / nari hate te /
kanashisa souru / aki no kure kana*

馴れ来にし都も疎く成果て悲しさ添ふる秋の暮かな

At a gathering where each person writes ten poems on autumn:

> Deep in the mountains
> mist fades in and out,
> never clearing up—
> faintly, I hear
> the voice of a deer.

Hare yara nu / miyama no kiri no / taedaeni /
honokani shika no / koe kikoyu nari

晴れやらぬ深山の霧の絶え絶えにほのかに鹿の声聞ゆなり

A distant mountain field
hidden
by clouds—
as autumn departs,
even to think of it is sad.

Kumo kakaru / tōyamabata no / aki sare ba /
omoi yaru dani / kanashiki mono wo

雲掛る遠山畑の秋去れば思ひ遣るだに悲しきものを

A DREAMLIKE WORLD

The ideograph for the word *hakanashi* (儚) has two elements: the left part means "human," and the right part means "dream." Taken together, this word means "passing," "fleeting," "fugitive," "transient," and "ephemeral," all of which are qualities reflected in Saigyō's poetry.

Japanese poetry depicts the world as *uki yo*, originally written as 憂世, meaning a "sad world," "gloomy world," "miserable world," or "suffering world." In time, *uki yo* was written as 浮世, meaning "floating world" and "fleeting world."

This all arose from the Buddhist teaching of impermanence (*mujō*, 無常), the literal meaning of which is "not always," "not permanent," which reflects the reality that nothing is unchanging. Nothing stays young and healthy. Nothing lives forever.

With all this in mind, you could say that Saigyō was a twelfth-century existentialist poet.

92*

I journeyed to Sanuku Province and looked for a trace of where Former Emperor Sutoku resided in exile. It was at a place called Tsu (port) in Matsuyama (Pine Mountain), but there was no remnant there at all.

> The appearance of waves
> at Pine Mountain
> hasn't changed—
> but you have become
> beyond form.

Matsuyama no / nami no keshiki wa / kawara ji wo /
kata naku kimi wa / nari mashi ni keri

松山の波の気色は変らじを形無く君はなりましにけり

93

How could months and years
have passed through this body—
someone who lived
in the world just yesterday
is no longer here today.

Toshi tsuki wo / ikade waga mi ni / okuri ken /
kinō no hito mo / kyō wa naki yo ni

年月を如何で我身に送りけん昨日の人も今日は無き世に

Even if you feel
that someone dead
is still alive—
know that this world
is but a sleeping dream.

Naki hito wo / aru wo omou mo / yononaka wa /
neburi no uchi no / yume to koso mire

亡き人も有るを思ふも世の中は眠りの中の夢とこそ見れ

95

ALL THINGS ARE IMPERMANENT

When I think of
the dreamlike past,
it's also true
right now—
dewdrops on the morning glory.

*Hakanaku te / sugi ni shi kata wo / omou ni mo /
ima mo sa koso wa / asagao no tsuyu*

儚くて過ぎにし方を思ふにも今も然こそは朝顔の露

96

Many years have passed.
I saw this small pine
in the garden so long ago—
I hear the sound of a storm
in its branches.

Mukashi mi shi / niwa no komatsu ni / toshi furi te /
arashi no oto wo / kozue ni zo kiku

昔見し庭の小松に年経りて嵐の音を梢にぞ聞

To get old
with no future,
how sad—
on the mountain's edge,
a pine broken by wind.

Oiyuke do / sue naki mi koso / kanashi kere /
katayamahata no / matsu no kazaore

老いゆけど末なき身こそ悲しけれ片山端の松の風折れ

When I lived in Saga, to the west of Kyōto, people got together to write poems about children playing.

> A bamboo horse—
> today I lean on it
> as a cane,
> remembering
> childhood games.

*Takeuma wo / tsue ni mo kyō wa / tanomu kana /
warabeasobi wo / omoiide tsutsu*

竹馬を杖にも今日は頼むかな童遊びを思ひ出でつゝ

99

Seeing a friend and longing for the past.

From now on
I'll be careful
speaking about the past—
mysteriously,
my sleeves grew moist.

Ima yori wa / mukashi gatari wa / kokorose n /
ayasiki made ni / sode shiore keri

今よりは昔語りは心せん妖しきまでに袖萎れけり

100

If I can't settle down
anywhere,
I'll just stay in the world
briefly,
like a brushwood hut.

Izuku ni mo / suma re zu ba tada / suma de ara n /
shiba no iori no / shibashi aru yo ni

何處にも住まれずば唯住まで有らん柴の庵の暫し有る世に

101[*]

A man from Kiso
couldn't drop anchor
in the raging sea—
he entered
the mountain of death.

Kiso bito wa / umi no ikari wo / shizume kane te /
shide no yama ni mo / iri ni keru kana

木曽人は海の碇を沈め兼ねて死出の山にも入りにけるかな

Warriors raised arms on this land; there is no place without battles—west, east, north, and south. I hear the increasing figure of those who have been killed is a great number. It's hard to believe. What is this fighting for? Feeling that this is a sorry state, I wrote this:

> There is no end
> to people
> starting across the mountain of death—
> the number of those killed
> keeps growing.

*Shide no yama / koyuru taema wa / ara ji kashi /
nakunaru hito no / kazu tsuzuki tsutsu*

死出の山越ゆる絶え間は有らじかし亡くなる人の数続きつゝ

103*

On the evening of the fifteenth (full moon) day of the seventh month, when the moon was shining, I visited Funaoka.

How can I hold on to
this evening's moon
so it shines
for those setting out
on the mountain's path of death?

Ikade ware / koyoi no tsuki wo / mi ni soe te /
shide no yamaji no / hito wo terasa n

如何で我今宵の月を身に添へて死出の山路の人を照らさん

104

While I ponder how old
my shadow has grown—
far off,
the moon
has already gone down.

Fuke ni keru / waga mi no kage wo / omou ma ni /
harukani tsuki no / katabuki ni keru

更けにける我身の影を思ふ間に遥かに月の傾きにける

105

The lamp also
loses the strength
to shine—
I'll just wait
until its light comes to an end.

Tomoshibi no / kakage-jikara mo / naku nari te /
tomaru hikari wo / matsu waga mi kana

灯火の掲げ力も無くなりて止まる光を待つ我身かな

106

When I resolve
to die
calmly—
my heart
echoes, Yes!

Uraurato / shina n zuru na to / omoitoke ba /
kokoro no yagate / sazo to kotau ru

遅遅と死なんずるなと思ひ解けば心の軈て然ぞと答ふる

LOVE

Love (*koi*, 恋) in Japanese poetry is romantic-erotic. It usually does not include compassion or family love. For Saigyō, love was a broken heart, longing, regret, and resentment. Although as a monk he was supposed to be free from love affairs, it was customary for any poet to write about imaginary love. Since some of Saigyō's love poems may not reflect his own actual experience or feelings, it is possible to see some of them as imagined.

107

LOVE

Streaming on the wind,
smoke rising from Mount Fuji
disappears in the sky—
there's no knowing
where my feelings go.

Kaze ni nabiku / Fuji no keburi no / sora ni kie te /
yukue mo shira nu / waga omoi kana

風に靡く富士の煙の空に消て行方も知らぬ我思哉

108

My love is
a slender
valley brook—
the sound of crashing rocks can be heard
downstream.

*Waga koi wa / hosotanigawa no / mizu nare ya /
sue ni iwa yaburu / oto kikoyu nari*

我恋は細谷川の水なれや末に岩破る音聞ゆなり

109

Parting After Making Love

> If we didn't hide
> being together,
> I wouldn't have to rise
> and leave earlier
> than dew on the grassy path.

Au koto wo / shinobi zari se ba / michi shiba no /
tsuyu yori sakini / oki te ko maji ya

逢ふことを忍ばざりせば道芝の露より先に起きて来まじや

Parting After Making Love

Robe over robe—
I hope the lingering scent
of mandarin flowers
will be strong this morning
before I depart.

*Kasane te wa / kokara mahoshi ki / utsuriga wo /
hana tachibana ni / kesa tague tsutsu*

重ねては濃からまほしき移り香を花橘に今朝蕎へつゝ

III

LOVE IN A DREAM

To meet
in a dream
has its limits—
if only there was no parting
when I awoke.

Au to miru / koto wo kagire ru / yumeji ni te /
samuru wakare no / nakara mashi kaba

逢ふと見る事を限れる夢路にて覚むる別れの無からましかば

112

The heart that admired
cherry blossoms
is distant now—
what remains
is an image of you.

Hana wo miru / kokoro wa yoso ni / hedatari te /
mi ni tsuki taru wa / kimi ga omokage

花を見る心は他所に隔たりて身に付きたるは君が面影

113

Why should I resent
someone who has grown
distant—
there were times for not being known,
and not knowing.

Utoku naru / hito wo nani to te / uramu ran /
shira re zu shira nu / ori mo ari shi ni

疎くなる人を何とて恨むらん知られず知らぬ折も有りしに

114

Without holding on to my dreams,
how could I have
endured these nights—
though you're not someone
I could ever meet again.

Yume wo nado / yogoro tanoma de / sugi ki ken /
sarade au beki / kimi nara naku ni

夢をなど夜ごろ頼まで過ぎ来けん然らで逢ふべき君なら無くに

115

Knowing my place,
I realize it's not her fault,
and yet—
pressed against my resentful face,
my sleeves are wet with tears.

Mi wo shire ba / hito no toga ni wa / omowa nu ni /
uramigao ni mo / nururu sode kana

身を知れば人の咎には思はぬに恨み顔にも濡るる袖哉

116

Day after day
my bitterness
grows—
the great ocean
of what I feel.

Hi ni soe te / urami wa itodo / ōumi no /
yutakanari keru / waga omoi kana

日に添へて恨みはいとど大海の豊かなりける我思ひ哉

117

Gazing upward
while being in love—
how my sadness
soaks in
the color of the moon!

Mono omoi te / nagamu ru koro no / tsuki no iro ni /
ikabakari naru / aware somu ran

物思ひて眺むる頃の月の色に如何ばかりなる哀れ染むらん

Because I grieve so deeply,
I try hard
to escape with my brush—
so much feeling
just can't be told.

Nageki amari / fude no susabi ni / tsukuse domo /
omou bakari wa / kaka re zari keri

嘆きあまり筆の遊みに尽せども思ふ許りは書かれざりけり

Neither asked
nor asking,
either way—
in my weary heart
pain is pain.

Towa re nu mo / towa nu kokoro no / tsurenasa mo /
uki wa kawara nu / kokochi koso sure

問はれぬも問はぬ心の強顔さも憂きは変らぬ心地こそすれ

I'll go now
to visit someone
in love—
I know the pain of loving
in this world!

*Ima wa ware / koise n hito wo / toburawa n /
yo ni uki koto to / omoishira re nu*

今は我恋せん人を訪はん世に憂き事と思ひ知られぬ

121

Now I understand—
"Promise
to remember . . ."
was her wish
to forget me.

Ima zo shiru / omoi ide yo to / chigiri shi ha
wasuren to te no / nasake nari keri

今ぞ知る思ひ出でよと契りしは忘れんとての情なりけり

122[*]

Do I remember
daybreak?
A cloud
lingers in the eastern sky,
reluctant to fade.

Ariake wa / omoide are ya / yokogumo no /
tada yoware tsuru / shinonome no sora

有明は思ひ出有れや横雲の只弱れつる東雲の空

LONELINESS

Even home leavers—monks and nuns—usually live in temples together. They have their own communities. Saigyō, by contrast, pushed himself to complete solitude. He had a visitor once in a while, and he occasionally visited others as well, but he was a master of being alone and a master of loneliness. Much of his poetry comes from his solitude.

Being alone means he always faced nature directly: the moon, the flowers, the trees, the birds, and the seasons. There was no one there but himself. In this way he got to know himself, was fully intimate with himself, and learned to get along with himself. A pure poet.

A goose flies off,
bearing white clouds
on its wings—
how it longs for its friends,
gathering by the rice field gate.

Shirakumo wo / tsubasa ni kake te / yuku kari no /
kadota no omo no / tomo shitau nari

白雲を翼に掛けて行く雁の門田の面の友慕ふなり

124

A pigeon
perches on a tree
in an ancient field—
calling out for a friend at dusk,
its voice is fierce!

Furuhata no / soba no tatsuki ni / iru hato no /
tomo yobu koe no / sugoki yūgure

古畑の傍の立つ木に居る鳩の友呼ぶ声の凄き夕暮

Even someone without much heart
knows loneliness.
A long bill snipe flies up
from the marsh—
autumn dusk.

Kokoro naki / mi nimo aware wa / shira re keri /
shigi tatsu sawa no / aki no yūgure

心無き身にも哀れは知られけり鴫立つ沢の秋の夕暮

Walking through piles of leaves
in the pure frosted garden—
how I long for someone
to come and ask,
"Have you seen the moon?"

Shimo sayu ru / niwa no konoha wo / fumi wake te /
tsuki wa miru ya to / tou hito mogana

霜冴ゆる庭の木の葉を踏み分けて月は見るやと訪ふ人もがな

It's lonely
in a mountain village
during the season of patchy showers—
the roar of a storm
grows strong.

*Yamazato wa / shigureshi koro no / sabishisa ni /
arashi no oto wa / yaya masari keri*

山里は時雨し頃の淋しさに嵐の音は稍々勝りけり

128

It's my heart
that makes my heart
feel longing—
this is how I make myself
suffer.

*Kokoro kara / kokoro ni mono wo / omowa se te /
mi wo kurushimu ru / waga mi nari keri*

心から心に物を思はせて身を苦しむる我身成けり

If someone else is suffering
from loneliness,
we might set our huts
side by side—
winter in a mountain village.

Sabishisa ni / tae taru hito no / mata mo are na /
iori narabe n / fuyu no yamasato

淋しさに堪へたる人の又も有れな庵並べん冬の山里

130

The loneliness
of this tumbling
thatched hut—
no one visits
but the wind.

Abare taru / kusa no ihori no / sabishisa wa /
kaze yori hoka ni / tou hito zo naki

荒れたる草の庵の淋しさは風より外に訪ふ人ぞ無き

131[*]

Lonely,
moonlight squeezes
into my hut—
on the mountain's rice field,
a bird-rattle makes the only sound.

Io ni moru / tsuki no kage koso / sabishi kere /
yamada wa hita no / oto bagari shi te

庵に洩る月の影こそ淋しけれ山田は引板の音ばかりして

132

When these flowers scatter,
and people return
to the capital—
this mountain may feel
so alone.

Hana mo chiri / hito mo miyako e / kaeri naba /
yama sabishiku ya / nara n to suru ran

花も散り人も都へ帰りなば山淋くやならんとするらん

133

Even when
there's no dark spot on the moon—
longing for someone
wears down my heart
and the moon.

Kuma mo naki / ori shimo hito wo / omoi ide te /
kokoro to tsuki wo / yatsushi tsuru kana

隈もなき折しも人を思い出でて心と月を窶しつるかな

134

Hiding behind my appearance
may become
more and more clear—
I'm not used
to so much longing.

Nakanakani / shinobu keshiki ya / shirukara n /
kakaru omoi ni / narai naki mi wa

中々に忍ぶ景色や著からん斯かる思に習ひ無き身は

To reach the point of so much misery—
why? Why
have I longed for someone
who won't accept me?
The years have just piled up!

Uki ni dani / nadonado hito wo / omoe domo /
kanawa de toshi no / tsumori nuru kana

憂きにだに何々人を思へども叶はで年の積りぬる哉

136

So much longing!
When I look at it
to soften what I feel—
moonlight
crushes my heart even more.

Koishisa ya / omoi yowaru to / nagamure ba /
itodo kokoro wo / kudaku tsukikage

恋しさや思ひ弱ると眺むればいとど心を砕く月影

Sent to a friend at the year's end:

> Although not expressing my love,
> it's comforting
> to wonder
> if someone longs for me—
> the year has come to an end.

Onozukara / iwa nu wo shitau / hito ya aru to /
yasurau hodo ni / toshi no kure nuru

自から言はぬを慕ふ人や有ると安らふ程に年の暮れぬる

Pine Tree in Front of My Hut

If I find it difficult
to stay here,
and drift away—
this pine
will be alone.

Koko wo mata / ware sumiuku te / ukare na ba /
matsu wa hitori ni / nara n to su ran

此処を又我住み憂くて浮れなば松は独りにならんとすらん

CORRESPONDENCE
AND CONVERSATIONS

Saigyō wrote poems solely in the *waka* form, consisting of thirty-one syllables. *Waka* was often written for self-reflection, but it was also used for correspondence both in high society and among home leavers. Messages of greetings, celebration, condolence, and love were communicated by sending a poem via a messenger. Lovers and married couples often wrote to each other in this way, as they lived separately in high society. In such a short form, wit, wordplay, hidden meanings, and reference to renowned poems were appreciated. Not to respond meant rejection. Often, replies were written on the spot and sent by messenger. These poetic conversations were marked by elegance and good taste.

Saigyō's correspondence verses include encouragement, condolence, consolation, invitations, and poems expressing affection or love to his fellow male practitioners.

To someone who had many reasons to serve in the imperial court but realized there was something more essential. After he went into seclusion at the Kiyomizu Temple upon entering a new year, I sent him this:

> May spring
> flourish
> along every branch—
> even on a withered tree,
> flowers bloom.

*Kono haru wa / edaeda made ni / sakayu beshi /
kare taru ki dani / hana wa saku meri*

この春は枝々迄に栄ゆべし枯れたる木だに花は咲くめり

Sent to someone who is supposed to serve in the court,
but instead is participating in a Buddhist retreat:

> It's also good
> not to live
> a worldly life
> beneath the autumn moon—
> it's filled with muddy water.

*Yo no nake ni / suma nu mo yoshi ya / aki no tsuki /
nigore ru mizu no / tatau sakari ni*

世の中に住まぬも良しや秋の月濁れる水の湛ふさかりに

141[*]

Āchārya Shōmei assembled one thousand people and held a Lotus Sūtra ceremony. Later I wrote to him:

> Since the old days
> when I joined,
> I realize not even a dewdrop
> of the dharma garden
> has changed.

Tsuranari shi / mukashi ni tsuyu mo / kawara ji to /
omoi shira re shi / nori no niwa kana

連なりし昔に露も変らじと思ひ知られし法の庭哉

After visiting the tomb of a woman, I wrote to her lover, thinking of what her soul might feel:

> While I think of the past,
> a storm of sadness
> comes down from the mountains—
> I wish someone would visit,
> even once in a while.

Omoiide te / miyamaoroshi no / kanashisa wo /
tokidoki dani mo / tou hito mo gana

思ひ出でて深山嵐の悲さを時々だにも訪ふ人もがな

Someone I had become close to said he was going to practice Buddhism in a faraway place. It was difficult to part, but he left. I wanted to show him maple leaves in their prime. I asked why he didn't come, despite my waiting. Thus, I wrote this while standing at the foot of the tree:

Deeply, I dyed my heart
the color
of maple leaves—
when we part
they will scatter and fall.

Kokoro wo ba / fukaki momiji no / iro ni some te /
wakare te yuku ya / chiru ni naru ran

心をば深き紅葉の色に染めて別れて行くや散るに成らん

144

I visited Kumano, Kii Province, in summer and stayed at a place on a river called Iwata. I sent this poem to Rev. Saijū in care of someone who traveled to Kyōto:

> At the foot of a pine
> on Iwata shore,
> an evening chill—
> I wish
> you were with me.

*Matsugane no / Iwata no kishi no / yūsuzumi /
kimi ga are na to / omohoyu ru kana*

松が根の岩田の岸の夕涼み君が有れなと思ほゆるかな

Hearing that Priest Saijū, who had traveled with me, was in seclusion at the Tennō Temple around the time of a full moon, I sent this:

> How much more
> than usual,
> with the moon
> setting in the west—
> I long for you.

Itodo ikani / nishi e katabuku / tsukikage wo /
tsune yori mo keni / kimi shitau ran

いとど如何に西へ傾く月影を常よりも異に君慕ふらん

146

While in retreat at a faraway place, I sent this poem to a friend in the capital city:

> The solitary moon,
> a memento
> high in the sky—
> if you remember,
> our hearts may travel across.

Tsuki no miya / uwa no sora naru / katami ni te /
omoi mo ide ba / kokoro kayowa n

月のみや上の空なる形見にて思ひも出でば心通はん

147*

To someone I was expecting to visit me at Mount Kōya in autumn but who didn't come, I sent this message after a snowfall:

> Buried in deep snow,
> I'm still hoping
> you will try to come—
> the mountain path is covered
> with a maple leaf brocade.

Yuki fukaku / uzumi te keri na / kimi ku ya to / momiji no nishiki / shiki shi yamaji wo

雪深く埋みてけりな君来やと紅葉の錦敷きし山路を

148*

Priest En'i (Saigyō) went up to Mudō Temple, saw Lake
Biwa from a room that extended out from the Daijō
Hall, and wrote this:

Grebes shining in the sun,
the lake calm
in the morning—
when I look far off,
a boat leaving no trace behind.

Nio teru ya / nagi taru asa ni / miwatase ba /
kogi yuku ato no / nami dani mo nashi

鳰照るや凪ぎたる朝に見渡せば漕ぎ行く跡の浪だにも無し

149*

Reply by Jien

In the faint light,
no trace of a boat
rowing on Ōmi Lake—
my heart
will follow that way.

*Honobonoto / Ōmi no umi wo / kogu fune no /
ato naki kata ni / yuku kokoro kana*

仄々と近江の海を漕ぐ舟の跡無き方に往く心かな

150*

Lady Junior Counselor, serving the Royal Nun, read
my collection of poems and commented:

> On each scroll
> a jewel-like voice
> speaks jewel-like phrases—
> though there might already
> have been something like this.

*Maki gotoni / tama no koese shi / tamazusa no /
tagui wa mata mo / ari keru mono wo*

巻毎に玉の声せし玉章の類は又も有けるものを

151

REPLY BY SAIGYŌ

If that's the case,
even when
they don't shine—
by calling them jewels
you may be polishing off dust.

Yoshi saraba / hikari naku tomo / tama to ii te /
kotoba no chiri wa / kimi migaka n

縦然らば光無くとも玉と言ひて言葉の塵は君磨かん

The moon was bright above the bridge at the inner shrine of Mount Kōya. I remembered having watched the moon together with Rev. Saijū at the same place, so I wrote to him in Kyōto:

> For no particular reason,
> I keep longing for you
> as I cross the bridge—
> moonlight is
> my only rival.

Koto to naku / kimi koi wataru / hashi no ue ni /
arasou mono wa / tsuki no kage nomi

事となく君恋ひ渡る橋の上に争ふ物は月の影のみ

153

Reply by Saijū

Without seeing
what's in my heart
as I think of you—
only moonlight is your rival
as you cross the bridge.

Omoi yaru / kokoro wa mie de / hashi no ue ni /
arasoi keri na / tsuki no kage nomi

思ひ遣る心は見えで橋の上に争ひけりな月の影のみ

Hearing that Priest Jakuchō was going to expound on
the dharma, I wrote to him:

> Though I'm not able
> to encounter
> your dharma—
> still, won't you count me
> among those who hear your name?

Hiromu ran / nori ni wa awa nu / mi nari tomo /
na wo kiku kazu ni / ira zara me yawa

弘むらん法には逢はぬ身なりとも名を聞く数に入らざらめやは

Reply by Jakuchō

Though this stream
has been heard
and transmitted—
you who draw dharma water
help it to gain in depth.

Tsutae kiku / nagare nari tomo / nori no mizu /
kumu hito kara ya / fukaku naru ran

伝へ聞く流れなりとも法の水汲む人からや深くなるらん

156*

When Lady Horikawa was living at Ninna Temple, I said I would visit her, but I was occupied with other things, and it took some time. About the time of a full moon, she heard that I had passed in front of the temple. She wrote:

> I depended on moonlight
> to guide me
> traveling west—
> how disappointing
> to trust in vain!

Nishi e yuku / shirube to tanomu / tsukikage no /
sora tanome koso / kai nakari kere

西へ行導と頼む月影の空頼めこそ甲斐無かりけれ

157

Reply by Saigyō

Not shining through,
moonlight
avoided the clouds—
it saw your heart
wasn't waiting in the sky.

Sashiira de / kumoji wo yoki shi / tsukikage wa /
mata nu kokoro zo / sora ni mie keru

射し入らで雲路を避きし月影は待たぬ心ぞ空に見えける

158

A lady of Kamisaimon'-in (the daughter of Emperor Toba and Empress Taikenmon'-in) visited Hōshō Temple for cherry blossom viewing, but it rained and dusk came on, so she went home. On another day, I wrote to Lady Hyōe (of Kamisaimon) to remind her of the imperial visit (by Emperor Toba and Empress Taikenmon'-in) in the past, saying:

> For those who see them,
> blossoms also must
> be thinking of the past—
> their longing
> withered by rain.

*Miru hito ni / hana mo mukashi wo / omoiide te /
koishikaru beshi / ame ni shioru ru*

見る人に花も昔を思ひ出でて恋しかるべし雨に萎るる

159

REPLY BY LADY HYŌE

Who would
see the rain
and long for the past?
Flowers also have no companions
from those days.

*Inishie wo / shinoburu ame to / tare ka mi n /
hana mo sono yo no / tomo shi nakere ba*

古へを偲ぶる雨と誰か見ん花もその世の友し無ければ

On the first anniversary of Former Empress Taiken-mon'in's passing, people gathered at her former abode. It was when the cherry blossoms on its southern front were falling. I wrote to Lady Horikawa who had served the empress:

> Even if we asked,
> the wind
> could not tell us where
> she has gone—
> the one who fell like a flower.

Tazunu tomo / kaze no tsute ni mo / kika ji kashi /
hana to chiri ni shi / kimi ga yukue wo

尋ぬとも風の伝にも聞かじかし花と散りにし君が行方を

161

REPLY BY HORIKAWA

If the blowing wind
would let me know
where she has gone—
I would not wait
to fall like a flower.

Fuku kaze no / yukue shira suru / mono nara ba /
hana to chiru ni mo / okure zara mashi

吹く風の行方知らする物ならば花と散るにも遅れざらまし

PURE LAND, SHINTŌ, AND DHARMA

At the age of sixty-eight, Saigyō witnessed a transition from the Heian (Kyōto) period to the Kamakura period, when a samurai government was established in Kamakura. He was associated with both major schools of Buddhism in the Heian period—the comprehensive Tendai School and Vajrayāna's Shingon School. He stayed at Mount Kōya, the center of Shingon, for some time.

Kamakura Buddhism, including the Pure Land and Zen schools, all of which advocated a wholehearted single practice, arose after Saigyō's death. However, continuous chanting of Amitābha Buddha's name by those wishing for rebirth in the Pure Land was already widely practiced. Saigyō was a part of this faith. It was natural for Buddhists to visit and pray at Japanese indigenous Shintō shrines whose deities are regarded as manifestations of buddhas.

162*

In this realm, when a person is focused on the Buddha's name, a lotus will grow in the western realm. If the person does not retreat from practice throughout life, this flower will come and welcome the person.

> I let the flower of my heart
> go before me
> to the pond of the western land—
> without forgetting this,
> I await the teaching of dharma.

*Nishi no ike ni / kokoro no hana wo / sakidate te /
wasure zu nori no / oshie wo zo matsu*

西の池に心の花を先立てて忘れず法の教へをぞ待つ

163

The Gadgada-svara Bodhisattva Chapter of the Lotus Sūtra says, "His face is as beautiful as millions of moons put together."

> My heart grows clear,
> serene in its light—
> just seeing
> one moon,
> on one night.

Waga kokoro / sayake ki kage ni / sumu mono wo / aru yo no tsuki wo / hitotsu miru dani

我心清けき影に澄む物を或る夜の月を一つ見るだに

164

All across this autumn field
moonlight shines—
polishing dewdrops
on petals
that sparkle like jewels.

Oshikome te / aki no no terasu / tsukikage wa /
hana naru tsuyu wo / tama ni migake ru

押し込めて秋の野照らす月影は花なる露を玉に磨ける

165*

So many fireflies
light up
the swampy marsh—
may my soul go
with them.

*Sawamizu ni / hotaru no kage no / kazu zo sou /
waga tamashii ya / yuki te gusu ramu*

沢水に蛍の影の数ぞ添ふ我魂や行きて具すらむ

I send my heart
beyond the mountain
where the moon sets—
what shall I do with the rest of me,
left in darkness?

Tsuki no yuku / yama ni kokoro wo / okuri ire te /
yami naru ato no / mi wo ikani se n

月の行く山に心を送り入れて闇なる跡の身を如何にせん

167

Upon Seeing a Painting of Hell

Though we keep
the sorry end of life
in mind—
how sad that we stray,
confused in this fleeting world.

Ukaru beki / tsui no omoi wo / oki nagara /
karisome no yo ni / madou hakanasa

憂かるべき終の思ひを置き乍ら仮初の世に惑ふ儚さ

It's rare
to rise into
human form—
who would not learn this,
only to sink down again?

Ukegataki / hito no sugata ni / ukabi ide te /
korizu ya dare mo / mata shizumu beki

受け難き人の姿に浮かび出て懲りずや誰も又沈むべき

169

The Immeasurable Life of the Tathāgata Chapter of the Lotus Sūtra

Vulture Peak—
one who perceives
the moon has disappeared
has a mind
that wanders in darkness.

Washi no Yama / tsuki wa iri nuru to / miru hito wa /
kuraki ni mayou / kokoro nari keri

鷲の山月は入りぬると見る人は暗きに迷ふ心なりけり

In response to the person who sent an iris to the temple
for use on the fifth day of the fifth month:

> I hang a green iris
> on the western side—
> in my heart
> this world's
> a temporary home.

*Nishi ni nomi / kokoro zo kakaru / ayame gusa /
kono yo wa kari no / yado to omoe ba*

西にのみ心ぞ掛る菖草この世は仮の宿と思へば

171

The Jeweled Tower Chapter of the Lotus Sūtra: "Those who keep the precepts and practice asceticism will quickly attain the unsurpassable Buddha Way."

I would have no oar
in the floating world
if there were no dharma—
the boat
of this moon.

Kai naku te / ukabu yo mo naki / mi nara mashi /
tsuki no mifune no / nori nakari se ba

櫂無くて浮かぶ世も無き身ならまし月の御舟の法無かりせば

Remembering a teaching that an aspiration for enlight-
enment is possible even in the flames of Avīchi hell:

> Even the torture
> of endless flames
> turns into enlightenment—
> if one's aspiration
> is raised.

*Hima mo naki / honoo no uchi no / kurushimi mo /
kokoro okose ba / satori ni zo naru*

暇もなき焔の中の苦しみも心発せば悟りにぞなる

With the roaring sound,
how could my heart
not become clear?
Grasses and trees bow down
in the storm.

Ikade ka wa / oto ni kokoru no / suma zara n /
kusaki mo nabiku / arashi nari keri

如何でかは音に心の澄まざらん草木も靡く嵐なりけり

174

THE BLISS OF MAKING AN OFFERING TO THE BUDDHA

Scattering
fragrant petals
before the enlightened one—
the wind
also knows my heart.

Hana no ka wo / satori no mae ni / chirasu kana /
waga kokoro shiru / kaze mo ari keri

花の香を悟りの前に散らすかな我心知る風も有りけり

The Parable of Herbs Chapter of the Lotus Sūtra: "I
see that all are equal. I do not harbor love and hatred to
these and those."

> Rice farmers don't hoard
> water
> for their seedlings alone—
> they let it flow in abundance
> downstream.

*Hikihikini / nawashiro mizu wo / wakeyara de /
yutakani nagasu / sue wo tōsa mu*

引き引きに苗代水を分けやらで豊かに流す末を通さむ

Flowing down,
the goddess crosses
the Shrine River—
sacred straw ropes
hang from the fence.

*Nagareide te / miato tare masu / mizugaki wa /
Miya Gawa yori ya / watarai no shime*

流れ出でて御跡垂れます瑞垣は宮河よりや度会の注連

The Mountain of Gods Path
has a pure moon
vow—
it shines
beneath the heavens.

Kamiji Yama / tsuki sayakanaru / chikai ari te /
ame no shita wo ba / terasu nari keri

神路山月清かなる誓ひ有りて天の下をば照らすなりけり

The Transformed Castle Chapter of the Lotus Sūtra:
"Shākyamuni Buddha attained unsurpassable enlight-
enment in the world of suffering."

> Was there a wish
> for the next night,
> to spread
> the full moon's light
> that set over Vulture Peak?

Omoi are ya / mochi ni hitoya no / kage wo soe te /
Washi no Miyama ni / tsuki no iri keru

思ひ有れや望に一夜の影を添へて鷲の御山に月の入りける

A ceaseless stream of waves
rules the world—
the divine wind
is fresh
on Mimosuso River's shore.

Nagare tae nu / nami ni ya yo wo ba / osamu ran /
kamikaze suzushi / Mimosuso no kishi

流れ絶えぬ波にや世をば治むらん神風涼し御裳濯の岸

How can the moon's
one light
in the sky
reflect in
uncountable dewdrops?

*Ika nare ba / sora naru kage wa / hitotsu ni te /
yorozu no mizu ni / tsuki yadoru ran*

如何なれば空なる影は一つにて万の水に月宿るらん

The Transformed Castle Chapter of the Lotus Sūtra:
"I vow to extend this merit so that all sentient beings
attain the Buddha Way together."

If we gathered all the dew
from each leaf
in an autumn field—
the water would fill
a lotus pond.

*Aki no no no / kusa no ha gotoni / oku tsuyu wo /
atsume ba hasu no / ike tatō beshi*

秋の野の草の葉毎に置く露を集めば蓮の池湛ふべし

182*

The Blissful Practice Chapter of the Lotus Sūtra: "Deeply entering *samādhi* and seeing buddhas of the ten directions."

> Deep in the mountains,
> the moon
> in your mind
> becomes a clear mirror—
> you see enlightenment all around.

Fukaki yama ni / kokoro no tsuki shi / sumi nure ba /
kagami ni yomo no /satori wo zo miru

深き山に心の月し澄みぬれば鏡に四方の悟りをぞ見る

183

The Bliss of the First Opening
of Lotus Blossoms

Would my heart
still
feel joy—
if the lotus hadn't blossomed
soon after I arrived?

Ureshisa no / nao ya kokoro ni / nokora mashi /
hodonaku hana no / hirake zari seba

嬉しさの尚や心に残らまし程なく花の開けざりせば

Dying my heart
with its color
in a single stroke—
a purple cloud
spreads above.

Hitosuji no / kokoro no iro wo / somuru kana /
tanabiki wataru / murasaki no kumo

一筋に心の色を染むるかな棚引き渡る紫の雲

185

The fragrance of wild peach in spring, and the color of thoroughwort (boneset) in autumn, are the reality of Samantabhadra Bodhisattva.

> Fields of color,
> spring fragrances—
> everything turns into enlightenment
> that soaks
> my heart.

Nobe no iro mo / haru no nioi mo / oshinabete /
kokoro some keru / satori to zo naru

野辺の色も春の匂ひも押し並べて心染めける悟りとぞなる

186

Devadatta Chapter of the Lotus Sūtra: "The World-honored One accepted the jewel the dragon woman offered."

Now I understand—
receiving a pearl
in the topknot
points to
polishing the mind.

Ima zo shiru / tabusa no tama wo / e shi koto wa /
kokoro wo migaku / tatoe nari keri

今ぞ知る髻の玉を得し事は心を磨く譬へなりけり

187*

I don't know
the other side of the mountain
where the sun sets—
before I leave, I will send my heart
to settle there.

*Irihi sasu / yama no anata wa / shira ne domo /
kokoro wo kane te / okuri oki tsuru*

入日さす山の彼方は知らねども心を予て送り置きつる

188

The Heart Sūtra

Keeping in my heart
the dharma
that all things are empty—
I shouldn't think for a moment
I am sinful.

Nanigoto mo / munashiki nori no / kokoro ni te /
tsumi aru mi to wa / tsuyu mo omawa ji

何事も空しき法の心にて罪ある身とは露も思はじ

189

Chanting the Buddha's Name at Dawn

Waking from my dream,
I merge with the sound
of the temple bell—
chanting the Buddha's name
ten times.

Yume samuru / kane no hibiki ni / uchisoe te /
totabi no mina wo / tonae tsuru kana

夢覚むる鐘の響きに打ち添へて十度の御名を唱へつる哉

190*

OBSERVING MIND

Darkness clears away,
the moon remains pure
in the sky of my heart—
the western mountain
may be drawing near.

*Yami hare te / kokoro no sora ni / sumu tsuki wa /
nishi no yamabe ya / chikaku naru ran*

闇晴れて心の空に澄む月は西の山辺や近くなるらん

191

The Five Hundred Disciples Chapter of the Lotus Sūtra

Polished naturally
by a pure heart,
I have learned to take out
the jewel of dharma
and put it on.

Onozukara / kiyoki kokoro ni / migaka re te /
tama toki kake kuru / nori wo shiri nuru

自から清き心に磨かれて玉解き掛けくる法を知りぬる

192*

With faith
in the Buddha's vow,
deep as the sea—
shall I not cross over
to the other shore?

*Wadatsuumi no / fukaki chikai ni / tanomi are ba /
kano kishibe ni mo / watara zara me ya*

海神の深き誓ひに頼み有れば彼の岸辺にも渡らざらめや

193

May my next life
reflect
what's in my heart—
light of
the timeless moon.

Komu yo ni wa / kokoro no uchi ni / arawasa mu /
aka de yami nuru / tsuki no hikari wo

来む世には心の中に現はさむ飽かで止みぬる月の光を

AN APPRECIATION:
SAIGYŌ AND THE WANDERING WAY

Those whose studies or practices are based on the spiritual and religious traditions that originally come from the East may find the opening words of the *Dao De Jing* somewhat familiar: "The Way that can be named is not the Way." It is certainly an eye-catching statement. But while there may be some ultimate truth in these words, my sense is that they should not be accepted without some careful examination regarding the verbal expression of the Way.

As a poet and monk whose wandering led him to traverse many a mountain and cross countless rivers in his lifetime of traveling the vast landscape of Japan until his death in 1190, Saigyō certainly gave eloquent voice to the Way as he found it, both in the external world he roamed and in the world of deep sentience within him. Indeed, the terrain Saigyō covered was not solely the physical landscape of Japan. Guided by his unusually sensitive heart and mind—the very personal attributes upon which his poems relied—he also journeyed deep within himself to end the attachments and delusions that beset him in this troubling and impermanent world. As he wrote, with no little affection and self-awareness, "Though I hold this world /dear, I cannot remain / attached— / only by forsaking the self / can I be free." It was not an easy task.

And so, with his Buddhist faith and sincere commitment to renunciation, Saigyō made a spiritual vow to free himself from suffering. Saigyō's poetry makes clear that in his wandering he fervently hoped to find a place, both in the world and within himself, "where misery can't be heard," and to enter the western paradise of enlightenment.

Always unpredictable and uncertain, Saigyō's wandering way often brought him the joys and pleasures of communing to the point of oneness with spring awakenings: the fragrance of budding plums wafting to the pillow where he slept in a temporary abode or the flowering of cherry blossoms so profoundly affecting the poet that he wrote he wished to die one day beneath a canopy of such plentiful blossoming "in the middle of spring / when the moon is full." It gave him great joy to make friends with mountain cuckoos and valley nightingales, to fall asleep to the song of nearby cicadas, and to play hide-and-seek with a deer who came to his hermitage. So fulfilling were Saigyō's experiences of oneness with other elements of the natural world that he lamented, "If this were a world, / where flowers never fell, / and clouds / didn't hide the moon— / I wouldn't worry about a thing."

But Saigyō's wandering showed him that such a world could not be found, so it also brought to him the unavoidable melancholic winds of autumn that foreshadowed death, making "everything ghostly" and "all things sad." This season, when the growing cold caused the sound of his cricket friends to become increasingly quiet and still until he could no longer hear them, often included fierce storms and isolating snows that led to a long winter seclusion, thus preventing Saigyō from having contact with friends and others for months at a time. It demanded that our poet face a daily and often lonely encounter with himself, absent even of the barest hope that another human being would brave the journey to the pathless, snowbound fragility of his brushwood hut. As he wrote, "The loneliness / of this tumbling / thatched hut— / no one visits / but the wind."

Huddling against the bitter storms in an abode where moonlight leaked in through the sparsely thatched roof and the rains formed puddles on the floor was the recurring reality that Saigyō knew all too well. It is no surprise, then, that even though he embraced his situation, he often found that a profound and undeniable existential loneliness was his most constant companion.

Saigyō's walking of the Way was clearly not an easy path to wander—not at all—but it was entirely his own. The external and internal worlds zigzagged into the unified landscape of his singular life; the words *inside* and *outside* lost all meaning as he sought to walk the Way of freedom that was "not near, not far"— as Shitou Xiqian wrote in his beloved eighth-century Chan poem "Sandōkai" ("The Merging of Relative and Absolute")— but from youth to old age could always be found right beneath his feet. He was a man guided by deep faith and a profound spiritual yearning that caused him to take up his wandering staff and embrace an extraordinary life of renunciation and artistic practice—yet his journey was a very ordinary type of extraordinary. He simply took one determined step at a time.

When You Walk the Way

So what is a path? What does it mean to walk the Way? Of course, we can say that it is an approach to living that others have practiced before, one that can be found by following the traces of writings, songs, chants, and teachings that others have left behind. And certainly this is one way we may find our path. Such artifacts are like the "broken branches" Saigyō bent when entering a deep mountain forest so he could find his way out again.

For Saigyō, however, the path was not simply something others had walked that could be readily followed; it was one he made himself, moment by moment, as seen in the spontaneous decisions and actions of his daily life, rooted in his deepest intentions, awareness, and understanding. In one poem, aware that he has chosen a solitary path that suits his natural inclinations, I can see him in a precarious situation high in the mountains, shaking his head with no small measure of self-reflective humor as he asks, "Who else / would search for cherry blossoms / on Mount Yoshino— / pressing ahead / on mossy rocks?"

Joy and privation were alternating visitors on Saigyō's path, and he embraced them equally. We glimpse in his poems a struggle with the sometimes-harsh inner landscape of his memories, thoughts, and feelings that often left him shaken yet persistent on his Buddhist path of liberation. He gives voice to this in one poem, where he writes, "Today's world / is a boat / with no place to anchor," and in another with "I would have no oar / in the floating world / if there were no dharma."

It is interesting to note that despite knowing that his chosen path was solely his own, toward the end of his life he did leave what he might have called a "broken branch" of a poem for those who might like to follow his example and seek to nourish lives of renunciation and solitude in nature—lives in which they might realize a measure of freedom and the miracle of their lives in this precious world: "From now on let me say / to those who wish / to see cherry blossoms— / renounce the world / and live in the mountains."

Some nine hundred years have passed since these poems were written. In all this time, and without any intention to serve as a model on Saigyō's part, his poetry has had a remarkable effect on readers. His simple, expressive style is so open and raw to the bone of human existence—of spiritual and corporeal yearning—that it still inspires people who seek the Way. Whether or not they take up the wandering staff, many follow Saigyō's path.

Among the most notable of Saigyō's followers was the beloved poet Bashō Matsuo, admired to this day for his exquisite haiku. His *Records of a Weather-Exposed Skeleton* and *Narrow Road to the North*, written five hundred years after Saigyō's time, have become classics over the centuries.

Bashō found Saigyō's poetic expression of the spontaneous encounter, his sideways glimpse into things as they are in their transparent but often unnoticed individual form, his articulation of the contemplative moment, and the playful exchange with his friends of the natural world so compelling that he embraced Saigyō's poetry as a north star for navigating his own life and poetry. It moved and encouraged him as he, too, faced the rigor and challenges of this impermanent existence and world. In fact, the extent to which he found Saigyō's poems a moving and profound source of inspiration caused Bashō to reverently acknowledge Saigyō as his poetic ancestor as he followed his own path and took to the road himself.

A Wandering Mind

In the parlance of our culture, and indeed of many cultures around the world, a wandering mind is not considered a positive attribute. It tends to indicate a mind that is unfocused, easily distracted, vague, and unproductive. In Saigyō's case, however, and for many other artists and spiritual practitioners of every description, the reality is quite the reverse. Free from habitual consideration, predictable and predigested thinking, the usual cultural associations, or simply what one has felt, thought, or even imagined before, the poet's wandering mind is so present, so unfettered, that it has a quality of nonaggressive alertness and receptivity. There is an eyes-open, ears-up not-knowing that is in every way receptive to the nuances of both the physical world and the contents of the heart and mind. It has a welcome openness to the subtle, ineffable world that may be experienced, for example, as a breeze that touches an arm in late summer, or the color and plenitude of cherry blossoms seen like never before against a fine blue spring sky. As the American poet Ezra Pound wrote in the opening lines of his "Canto CXX," "I have tried to write Paradise / Do not move / Let the wind speak / that is paradise."

Here we encounter that wandering mind, the mind that knows how to let the wind speak and be experienced as it lightly brushes the skin without the interruption of human thinking. Slight and soft as this touch may be, when the mind is so disposed to receive it just as it is, meaning may be created; realization may be found.

This wandering mind is a disposition toward the world of unknowing, or not-knowing. It has trained itself to allow full and intimate immersion with whatever it encounters. It is the mind of poet and seeker alike, both of whom know, even if only for an instant, that whatever one encounters is the self.

In a story from the Zen tradition that readers may recall, one day two teachers meet. One of them is carrying her bags, so the other teacher asks her where she is going. "I'm going on a pilgrimage," she replies. Hoping to inquire further, the first teacher asks, "And what is the purpose of pilgrimage?" The second teacher responds truthfully, with perhaps a bit of a sparkle in her eye since she has immediately caught the nature of the penetrating question. "I don't know," she says. "Ah," the first teacher responds, "not-knowing is most intimate."

Unquestionably, based on the evidence of his poetry, this was Saigyō's mind. It allowed him to experience the oneness and serenity found in realization or in his feeling of intimacy with the cherry blossoms he found so dear that he climbed mountain paths just to be with them for a while. It helped him to fearlessly explore the depths of his thought and feeling as he worked with his aspiration to be free from all that made him suffer, including his own internal world. After all, with insight typical of the poet, he well knew that "It's my heart / that makes my heart / feel longing— / this is how I make myself / suffer."

While Saigyō certainly wrote the poems in this volume, there is a way in which they do not belong solely to him. Natural, simple, expressive, authentic, and true, they arise from the mind that received them, but they speak for so many others at the same time. This points to what the poet John Keats meant when he wrote "the reader completes the poem." When poets give themselves as completely as Saigyō did to the world he wandered while walking the Way, what emerges becomes a universal expression.

For centuries readers have been touched, not only by what the poet experienced and put into words, but by a kind of personal recognition within themselves, where *re-* means "again" and *cognition* can mean "knowing." To read Saigyō is to know again what we may have always known in some deep part of ourselves but not realized until that knowing was awakened and nourished by the poetry. The poems may even take us from the world of knowing to a place that can be experienced as beyond knowing; a place completely outside language that is experienced by poetry lovers and seekers of the Way alike. Is this not a treasure indeed?

—PETER LEVITT

Acknowledgments

Our deep appreciation goes to Samuel Bercholz, the founder of Shambhala Publications. In 1967–69, Peter lived in a small building in the Mission District of San Francisco, shared by Sam and Hazel who lived upstairs. From time to time, they'd sit on the front steps and talk about Buddhism. One day Sam came home from Berkeley and with no little excitement told Peter that he had been given permission to sell some books at the back of a bookstore on Telegraph Avenue, and he was going to call his little spot Shambhala. The virtues of a humble beginning, and the benefits to many, could not be clearer! Kaz's first book in the United States, *Enku: Sculptor of a Hundred Thousand Buddhas*, was published by Shambhala in 1982. Peter and Kaz have gratefully been collaborating with Sam separately and together over four decades.

We offer our thanks to Nikko Odiseos for accepting our manuscript and leading this book project. We are also grateful to Peter Schumacher for his excellent editing. It has been our pleasure to work with our assistant editor Samantha Nicole Ripley and our wonderful designer Lora Zorian. Our thanks also go to all of the Shambhala staff who helped to make this book possible.

Peter also extends a deep-hearted thanks to his wife, the poet Shirley Graham, for her insight, support, and enjoyment of these translations as they were brought into English.

Kaz thanks Susan O'Leary and Roberta Werdinger for their excellent editorial advice. He also thanks Yuka Saito for working on the bibliography. Linda Hess gave him advice as always and kindly hosted Peter and Shirley when they visited Berkeley.

Our thanks, as well, to Victoria Shoemaker for representing Kaz and to Anne Edelstein for representing Peter.

PETER LEVITT AND KAZUAKI TANAHASHI

Notes

67 Saga is a village west of Kyōto.

68 See page 43 of the Introduction.

69 Shirakawa, meaning "White River," is a brook that runs through Kyōto.

70 See note 59.

84 Miyagi No, or "Miyagi Field," is in Mutsu Province, in the far northeast of the country.

85 Ikoma Peak is a mountain bordering Yamato and Settsu Provinces (present-day Nara and Ōsaka Prefectures).

89 Jakunen was a young monk and friend of Saigyō's. Formally a courtier, Yorihira Fujiwara. Dates of birth and death unknown.

92 See page 16 of the Introduction.

101 Yoshinaka Minamoto, from Kiso County in Shinano Province, was a commander of the Minamoto clan. He was killed by other Minamoto troops in a battle east of Kyōto in 1184. See page 19 of the Introduction.

103 Funaoka is a hill north of Kyōto.

110 The poet wishes to lay his robe over his lover's so he can take away a lingering scent when they part. It was customary to exchange inner robes after making love for the first time.

122 Remembering his departure from a lover in the morning.

131 A bird-rattle is made of a small board and thin bamboo pipes connected to a rope. It is meant to be pulled by a farmer. As with a scarecrow, bird-rattles are used to dissuade birds from eating seeds or grains.

139 Kiyomizu Temple is a joint practice place of the Hossō (Dharma Characteristics) and Shingon schools, located at the foot of the East Mountain Range of Kyōto.

141 Āchārya is a title for a Vajrayāna Buddhist master.

145 It is said that the western paradise can be fully viewed from the west gate of the Tennō Temple in the city of Naniwa.

147 Mount Kōya, in Kii Province, is the center of Vajrayāna's Shingon School.

148 This is a verse by Saigyō for Jien found in Jien's anthology *Shūgyoku Shū*.

149 See note 148.

150 A daughter of Shinzei Fujiwara (1106–1160), Lady Junior Counselor served the royal nun Kenshummon'-in (1142–1176), the former empress of Emperor Goshirakawa.

156 Saigyō means "traveling west" or "going west."

162 Saigyō's headnote is a quotation from a prayer in a ceremony for chanting the Buddha's name.

165 There is a folk belief that one's soul (*tamashii*) is in the shape of a ball (*tama*) that floats in the air.

170 There was a custom that on the fifth day of the fifth month, known as the Boy's Day Festival, people would hang irises from the eaves of a house to rid it of evil spirits. The plant, with its fresh scent, is also used in the bath.

172 Avīchi (Sanskrit) is the hell of endless suffering.

175 Whether for a nursery or for transplantation, rice farmers filled their fields first and then sent the rest of the water to be used by the farmers downstream.

176 According to legend, the sun goddess Amaterasu crossed this river and settled beside it in Ise Province. Therefore, it is called Miya Gawa, which means "Shrine's River." It is also called "Isuzu Gawa" or "Mimosuso Gawa." Straw ropes with hanging strips of folded white paper

are called *shime-nawa* and are used to mark a sacred boundary.

177 Kamiji Yama (Mountain of Gods Path) stands by the Ise Shrine in Ise Province.

178 The fifteenth day of the month in the lunar calendar is the night of the full moon. Here, Saigyō wonders if Shākyamuni Buddha's enlightenment includes the next night and all other nights with a vow to save all beings.

179 The Ise Shrine is on Mimosuso River, also called Isuzu River, or Shrine River.

182 *Samādhi* (Sanskrit) is a one-pointed state of body, mind, and heart in meditation.

184 Purplish gold symbolizes the Buddha's body.

187 Saigyō's thought of the western paradise.

190 The Pure Land is believed to be beyond the western mountains.

192 Wadatsumi is the god of the ocean in Shintōism. But this poem seems to refer to a vow by Amitābha Buddha to bring sentient beings to the shore of enlightenment.

Bibliography

English

Brower, Robert H., and Earl Miner. *Fujiwara Teika's Superior Poems of Our Time*. Stanford, CA: Stanford University Press, 1967.

Honda Heihachirōo. *The Sanka Shū*. Tōkyō: The Hokuseidō Press, 1971.

LaFleur, William R. *Awesome Nightfall: The Life, Times, and Poetry of Saigyō*. Somerville, MA: Wisdom Publications, 2012.

McKinney, Meredith. *Gazing at the Moon: Buddhist Poems of Solitude*. Boulder, CO: Shambhala Publications, 2021.

Saigyō, *Saigyō: Poems of a Mountain Home*, translated by Burton Watson. New York: Columbia University Press, 1991.

Japanese

Arashiyama Kōzaburō. *Saigyō to Kiyomori* [Saigyō and Kiyomori]. Tōkyō: Shūei Sha, 1992.

Hisamatsu Sen'ichi, et al. *Shinkokin Waka Shū* [Shinkokin Waka Anthology]. Tōkyō: Iwanami Shoten, 1958.

Inoue Muneo. *Waka no Kaishaku to Kanshō Jiten* [Dictionary of Interpretation and Appreciation of Waka]. Tōkyō: Ōbun Sha, 1979.

Inoue Yasushi. *Saigyō: Sanka Shū, Gendaigoyaku Nihon no Koten 9*. Tōkyō: Gakken, 1981.

Jun. *Kokin Shū, Shinkokin Shū. Zusetsu Nihon no Koten #4* [Kokin Syū and Shinkokin Shū, Illustrated Japanese Classical Literature 4]. Tōkyō: Shūei Sha, 1979.

Kazamaki Keijirō and Kojima Yoshio. *Sanka Shū, Kinkai Waka Shū* [Sanka Shū and Kinkai Waka Shū]. Tōkyō: Iwanami Shoten, 1961.

Kubota Jun and Yoshino Tomomi. *Saigyō Zenkashū* [Entire Collection of Saigyō's Waka]. Tōkyō: Iwanami Shoten, 2013.

Kuwabara Hiroshi. *Saigyō Monogatari* [Saigyō Stories]. Tōkyō: Kōdan Sha, 1981.

Kuwako Toshio. *Saigyō no Fūkei* [Landscape of Saigyō]. Tōkyō: NHK Shuppan, 1999.

Mezaki Tokue. *Saigyō*. Tōkyō: Yoshikawa Kōbun Kan, 1980.

Nishizawa Yoshihito. *Saigyō: Tamashī no Tabiji* [Saigyō: Journey of the Soul]. Tōkyō: Kadokawa Shoten, 2010.

Shirane Haruo, et al. *Sekai e Hiraku Waka: Gengo, Kyōdōtai, Jendā* [Waka Opening Up to the World: Language, Community, and Gender]. Tōkyō: Bensei Syuppan, 2012.

Shirasu Masako. *Saigyō*. Tōkyō: Shinchō Sha, 1996.

Suzuki Hiroko. *Kokin Waka Shū no Sōzōryoku* [Imaginative Power of Kokin Waka Anthology]. Tōkyō: NHK Shuppan, 2018.

Takahashi Hideo. *Saigyō*. Tōkyō: Iwanami Shoten, 1993.

Tsuji Kunio. *Saigyō Kaden* [Saigyō Flower Transmission]. Two volumes. Tōkyō: Shinchō Sha, 1995.

Tsunoda Bunei. *Taikenmonin Shōshi no Shōgai: Shōtei Hishō* [Life of Taikenmonin Shōshi: Secret of the Fragrant Garden]. Tōkyō: Asahi Shimbun Shuppan, 1985.

Ueda Miyoji. *Saigyō, Sanetomo, Ryōkan* [Saigyō, Sanetomo, and Ryōkan]. Tōkyō: Kadokawa Shoten, 1979.

Yoshimoto Taka'aki. *Saigyō Ron* [Discussions on Saigyō]. Tōkyō: Kōdan Sha, 1990.

INDEX OF THE FIRST LINES
AND SOURCES

First line is followed by poem number and source.

About the Translators

PETER LEVITT's numerous books of poetry, prose, and translation include *One Hundred Butterflies*; *Fingerpainting on the Moon: Writing and Creativity as a Path to Freedom*; and with Kazuaki Tanahashi, *The Essential Dogen: Writings of the Great Zen Master* and *The Complete Cold Mountain: Poems of the Legendary Hermit Hanshan*. He also authored *Yin Mountain: The Immortal Poetry of Three Daoist Women*, translated with Rebecca Nie. In 1989 he received the Lannan Foundation Award in Poetry. He is the founding teacher of the Salt Spring Zen Circle in British Columbia, where he lives with his wife, the poet Shirley Graham.

KAZUAKI TANAHASHI was born in Japan in 1933 and has been active in the United States since 1977. He coauthored *The Complete Cold Mountain: Poems of the Legendary Hermit Hanshan* and *The Essential Dogen: Writings of the Great Zen Master* with Peter Levitt. He also wrote *Sky Above, Great Wind: Life and Poetry of Zen Master Ryokan* and *Painting Peace: Art in a Time of Global Crisis*. His latest publication is *Gardens of Awakening: A Guide to the Aesthetics, History, and Spirituality of Kyōto's Zen Landscapes*, with photos by Mitsue Nagase.